Myrc's
Instructions for Parish Priests.

DUBLIN: WILLIAM McGEE, 18, NASSAU STREET.
EDINBURGH: T. G. STEVENSON, 22, SOUTH FREDERICK STREET.
GLASGOW: M. OGLE & CO., 1, ROYAL EXCHANGE SQUARE.
BERLIN: ASHER & CO., UNTER DEN LINDEN, 20.
NEW YORK: C. SCRIBNER & CO. LEYPOLDT & HOLT, 451, BROOME ST.
PHILADELPHIA: J. B. LIPPINCOTT & CO.
BOSTON U.S.: DUTTON & CO.

Instructions for Parish Priests

By

John Myrc.

edited by

Edward Peacock

Second revised edition

EARLY ENGLISH TEXT SOCIETY

Original Series, 31

1868

Second revised edition

1902

KRAUS REPRINT CO.
Millwood, New York
1975

Unaltered reprint 2000
ISBN 0 85991 818 1
Distributed for the Early English Text Society by
Boydell & Brewer Ltd, PO Box 9, Woodbridge, Suffolk IP12 3DF
and Boydell & Brewer Inc, PO Box 41026, Rochester, NY 14604-4126
Printed and bound in Great Britain by Antony Rowe Ltd, Chippenham, Wiltshire

Instructions for Parish Priests.

By John Myrc.

EDITED FROM COTTON MS. CLAUDIUS A. II.,

BY

EDWARD PEACOCK, F.S.A., &c.

[*Revised 1902.*]

LONDON:
PUBLISHED FOR THE EARLY ENGLISH TEXT SOCIETY,
BY KEGAN PAUL, TRENCH, TRÜBNER & Co., LTD.

MDCCCLXVIII.

1 *

31.

HERTFORD:

PRINTED BY STEPHEN AUSTIN.

PREFACE.

The poem, now printed for the first time, has been preserved in at least three manuscripts. The best of these, as giving the earliest and purest text, is the one in the British Museum,[1] from which the present imprint is made. It was written out, in the editor's opinion, not later than the year 1450, perhaps a little earlier; but the language is of a somewhat older date. The other two manuscripts are among the late Mr. Douce's collections in the Bodleian Library.[2] These differ frequently, but seldom materially, from the London copy. They are of later execution, and show a tendency to the vocabulary of the north country in their variations. They are not the handy-work of the same scribe, but the texts are so nearly identical that there can be little doubt that they have both been copied from one original. All the various readings that seemed of any interest have been noted. It was not desirable to record every difference of spelling.

Of the writer of the work nothing is known, except that he was a Canon of Lilleshall, in Shropshire, a house founded by Richard de Belmeis, between 1144 and 1148, for a body of Arroasian canons. They were a branch of the order of canons regular of St. Austin, who took their name from the

[1] Cotton MS., Claud. A. ii.

[2] Douce MSS., 60 and 103.

city of Arras, near which their first house, dedicated to St. Nicholas, was situated. The offshoot of which Mirk was in due time a member had, in its early days, many migrations. The first English home of the brotherhood seems to have been at a place called Lizard Grange. They afterwards occupied for a time some houses at Donnington Weald, whence they moved to Dorchester, where they seem to have remained until their permanent home was fitted for their reception. Here they continued to reside until the suppression of the monastic orders. The site of the Abbey was granted by Henry the Eighth, in the thirty-first year of his reign, to James Leveson. Some remains still exist to show that the church was a Norman building of fine proportions.[1]

Mirk was the author of another book, also in English, which is well worthy the attention of those who take an interest in our earlier literature. A copy is preserved in the same volume from which this imprint is taken. Its title is *Liber Festivalis*. It consists of a collection of Sermons for the higher festivals of the Christian year, beginning with the first Sunday in Advent.

Mirk tells us that he translated this poem from a Latin book called *Pars Oculi*. Some people have therefore thought that it is a versified translation of John De Burgo's *Pupilla Oculi*. Such a suggestion can only have been made by persons whose acquaintance with the books was limited to their titles. De Burgo's book is probably twenty times as large, and is as different from Mirk's verses as a book well can be that treats in part upon similar subjects.

The *Manuale Sacerdotis* of Johannes Miræus, prior of Lilleshall, has also been conjectured to be the origin from which Mirk translated.[2] The prior's book is much like the monk's,

[1] Monast. Anglic., vi. 261; Coll. Arch., i. 28; Pitseus, 577.
[2] There is a manuscript of this work in the Harleian Library, No. 5306.

both in subject and method of treatment, but it is much larger, and, in other ways, quite an independent work.

Although we cannot at present put our hands upon the original Latin text from which the version before us was made, it is quite evident that there is very little that is original about it. How could there be? The author was treating on subjects that were as old as the Christian Church, and giving directions how priests with little book-learning or experience were to teach the faith to their flocks. Great numbers of independent works of this nature were produced in the Middle Ages. There is probably not a language or dialect in Europe that has not now, or had not once, several treatises of this nature among its early literature. The growth of languages, the Reformation, and the alteration in clerical education, consequent on that great revolution, have caused a great part of them to perish or become forgotten.

A relic of this sort, fished up from the forgotten past, is very useful to us as a help towards understanding the sort of life our fathers lived. To many it will seem strange that these directions, written without the least thought of hostile criticism, when there was no danger in plain speaking, and no inducements to hide or soften down, should be so free from superstition. We have scarcely any of the nonsense which some people still think made up the greater part of the religion of the Middle Ages, but, instead thereof, good sound morality, such as it would be pleasant to hear preached at the present day.

The instructor tells his pupils of the great evil it is to have ignorant clergy, how instead of instructing their people they by their ill example lead them into sin. How their preaching is worth but very little if they tell lies or get drunk, are slothful, envious, or full of pride. How they may not without sin haunt taverns, or practice violent and cruel sports;

may not dance nor wear "cutted clothes and pyked schone"; nor go to fairs and markets, and strut about girt with sword and dagger like knights and esquires. On the other hand, he says priests must be gentle and modest, given to hospitality, and the reading of the psalter. They must avoid as much as may be the service of women, and especially of evil ones; eschew coarse jokes and ribald talking, and must be especially careful to shave the crown of their heads and their beards.

The priest must not be content with simply knowing his own duties. He must be prepared to teach those under his charge all that Christian men and women should do and believe. We are told that when anyone has done a sin he must not continue long with it on his conscience, but go straight to the priest and confess it, least he should forget before the great shriving-time at Eastertide. Pregnant women especially are to go to their shrift and receive the holy communion at once. Our instructor is very strict on the duties of midwives—women they were really in those days. They are on no account to permit children to die unbaptized. If there be no priest at hand, they are to administer that sacrament themselves if they see danger of death. They must be especially careful to use the right form of words, such as our Lord taught; but it does not matter whether they say them in Latin or English, or whether the Latin be good or bad, so that the intention be to use the proper words. The water and the vessel that contained it are not to be again employed in domestic use, but to be burned or carried to the church and cast into the font. If no one else be at hand, the parents themselves may baptize their children. All infants are to be christened at Easter and Whitsuntide in the newly blessed fonts, if there have not been necessity to administer the sacrament before. God-parents are to be careful to teach to their god-children the *Pater Noster*, *Ave Maria*, and *Credo*, and not to sleep in the same bed with them until they are old enough to take care of themselves, lest they should be overlain. Neither are they to be sponsors to their god-children at confirmation, for they have already contracted a spiritual relationship. Both the god-parents and those who have held the child at its confirming are spiritual relatives, and may not afterwards contract marriage with it.

Before weddings, banns are to be asked on three holidays; and all persons who contract irregular marriages, and the priests, clerks, and others that help thereat, are cursed for the same. The real presence of the body and blood of our Saviour in the Sacrament of the Altar is to be fully held; but the people are to bear in mind that the wine and water given to them after they have received Communion is not a part of the sacrament. It is an important thing to behave reverently in church, for the church is God's house, not a place for idle prattle. When people go there they are not to jest, or loll against the pillars and walls, but kneel down on the floor and pray to their Lord for mercy and grace. When the gospel is read they are to stand up and sign themselves with the cross; and when they hear the sanctus bell ring, they are to kneel and worship their Maker in the blessed sacrament.

Not a word is said by Mirk indicating that he knew anything about pews or even benches for the lay people. It is probable that these conveniences were not commonly needed at the time when he wrote.

All men are to show reverence when they see the priest carrying the Host to the sick. Whether the ways be dirty or clean they are not to think of their clothes, but reverently to kneel down to "worshype Hym that alle hath wroghte."

The author gives some very interesting instructions about

churchyards, which show, what we knew from other circumstances to be the case, that they were sometimes treated with shameful irreverence. It was not for want of good instruction that our ancestors, in the days of the Plantagenets, played at rustic games, and that the gentry held their manorial courts over the sleeping-places of the dead. That then, as seventy years ago,—as now perhaps—

> "dogs and donkeys, sheep and swine,
> The clerk's black mare, the parson's kine,
> Among the graves their pastime take;
> That at the yearly village wake
> Each man and woman, lad and lass,
> Do play at games upon the grass;
> Set curs to fight and cats to worry,
> And make the whole place hurry-skurry."

Of witchcraft we hear surprisingly little. Mirk's words are such that one might almost think he had some sceptical doubts on the subject. Not so with usury or "okere." The taking interest for money, or lending anything to get profit thereby, is, we are shown, a "synne full greuus." This was the universally received teaching in his day, and for many centuries after. Perhaps the most remarkable fluctuation of opinion that has taken place in the modern period, is the silent change that has passed over men's minds on this important subject.

After these and several more general instructions of a similar character, almost all of them showing good religious feeling and clear common-sense, the author gives a very good commentary on the Creed, the Sacraments, the Commandments, and the deadly sins. The little tract ends with a few words of instruction to priests as to the manner of saying mass, and of giving holy communion to the sick.

When the editor first read this little book, in one of the Oxford manuscripts, it was his intention to print it with an extended commentary, for the purpose of illustrating the ritual, religious, and social feelings of an important period in history. This would have been out of place in a publication of the Early English Text Society. The document as it stands speaks clearly enough to those to whom its voice is audible.

As an illustration of Mirk's work the editor has printed from Lansdowne MS., 762, seven questions to be asked of persons near death. The date of the manuscript from which they are taken is thought to be about 1470. The volume is written partly on vellum and partly on paper, and contains many different pieces. Several of them are prophesies.

The editor must not conclude without thanking his learned friend John Ross, Esq., of Lincoln, for his many valuable notes and suggestions; especially for the interesting extracts concerning ankresses, from his unrivalled collections relative to the history of this his native county. He has also received kind help from the Very Reverend Daniel Rock, D.D.; and from his friends James Fowler, Esq., F.S.A., of Wakefield, and the Reverend Joseph T. Fowler, F.S.A., of St. John's College, Hurstpierpoint.

E. P.

BOTTESFORD MANOR, NEAR BRIGG.
September 9, 1867.

AFTERWORDS.

July 21, 1902.—This Text having been long out of print, and Mr. Peacock not having leisure to revise it, I have read it again with the MS., shifted the "Cursing" to its proper place, and printed it from the longer and better Cotton MS. I have also added a couple of notes, and made a few corrections in the Notes and Glossary.

The frequent occurrence of the full form 'Ihesus' in this MS. (and elsewhere) justifies the extension of the usual contraction Ih̄us as Ih*e*sus, though objection has been made to it that the *e* is already represented by the *h̄*. But the fact that *h* stood for *e* was not known by the early English scribes.

F. J. FURNIVALL.

Erratum.—P. 64, l. 1: *for* 'do lyueraunce' *read* 'de-lyueraunce.'

CONTENTS.

CORRECTIONS FOR E. E. T. SOC., ORIG. SER., No. 31, MYRC'S INSTRUCTIONS FOR PARISH PRIESTS.

By H. P. Lee.

NOTES.

p. 73, l. 31. *Dronkelewe* is the adjectival form,—given to drinking.

p. 82, l. 353. A.S. *nyten*, or *nēat*, is from *nēotan*, to be useful.

„ l. 360. *Telyng* (lit. tilling) means sorcery; cf. Tele, l. 368, which may = Tile; the idea being—cultivation, study, sorcery (Stratmann).

p. 83, l. 419. *Gult* is the p. part. of gülten, to sin.

p. 88, l. 1175. *Wedde: delete* (from Goth. *With-an*, &c.): *add* cf. Goth. *wadi*, Lat. *vas* (gen. *vadis*), a pledge.

GLOSSARY.

A-bygge, 59/1898, *read* pay for.

Bollyng, 11 note, *read* (more probably) playing ball.

Churchay, 11 note, *delete* "*Heg*, hay, grass, or."

Elynge, þe laste ——, 17/533, *read* extreme unction.

Fere, 13/407, *read* sound, *lit.* able to go.

Frechedly, 38/1220, *read* greedily: cf. Mirk's Festial, 84/1.

Gryth, 49/1581; *read* peace, security.

Gult, 13/419; *read* sinned.

Halybred, 42/1346; *read* the holy bread: *delete* "*eulogia.*"

Helet, 29/942; *read* hidden.

Hodymoke, 59/1919; *read* secrecy: cf. *in hudeloke* (for which the text may be a scribe's error) in Mirk's Festial, 159/32.

Laske, 50/1624; *read* relax.

Layne, 22/698, 43/1398; *read* denial.

Lyde ȝate, 43/1385; *read* lidgate, postern (Stratmann).

Lyth, 39/1253; *read* limb.

Mynge, 45/1443, 59/1915; *delete* "mingle" and "*mengian*": *add* A.S. *myngian* = *myndgian*, to bear in mind.

Myscheueth, 17/550; *read* comes to harm.

Nyse, 3/61; foolish.

Nyste, 37/1209; *read* folly. O.Fr. *nicete;* cf. *nyse*, 3/61, and *nysete*, Macro Pl. 57/654.

Nythinge, 36/1173; *read* A.S. *nīþing.*

Prow, 17/548; *read* O.Fr. *prou.*

Sybbe, 22/718; *read* A.S. *sibb*, *godsibb.*

Tele, 12/368 }
Telynge, 12/360 } See Revised Notes.

Þonkes, þy ——, 24/779; *read* of thy own will, voluntarily: cf. Chaucer, Knightes Tale, ll. 1626, 2114.

Vys, 38/1225; *read* device. O.Fr. *devis*, *vise.*

Weynt, be ——, 34/1102; *read* turned away. A.S. *bewendan.*

Wyntynge, 13/397; *read* Wytynge.

Yeke, 10/322; *read* Ylke.

ȝore, 1/9; *read* long ago.

Instructions for Parish Priests.

COTTON. MS. CLAUDIUS A II. FOL. 127.

¶ Propter presbiterum parochialem instruendum.

GOd seyth hym self, as wryten we fynde,
That whenne þe blynde ledeth þe blynde,
In-to þe dyche þey fallen boo,
For þey ne sen whare by to go.
So faren prestes now by dawe;
They beth blynde in goddes lawe,
That whenne þey scholde þe pepul rede
In-to synne þey do hem lede.
Thus þey haue do now fulle ȝore,
And alle ys for defawte of lore,
Wharefore þou preste curatoure,
Ȝef þou plese thy sauyoure,
Ȝef thow be not grete clerk,
Loke thow moste[1] on thys werk;
For here thow myȝte fynde & rede.
That þe be-houeth to conne nede,
How thow schalt thy paresche preche.
And what þe nedeth hem to teche,
And whyche þou moste þy self be.
Here also thow myȝte[2] hyt se;
For luytel ys worthy þy prechynge,
Ȝef thow be of euyle lyuynge.

When the blind lead the blind both fall into the ditch.

Priests lead their flocks into sin through their own want of lore.

Ignorant priests should read this book.

Preaching worth little if the preacher's life be evil.

[1] oft. [2] myghtest.

Priests must be chaste,

Preste,[1] þy self thow moste be chast,
And say þy serues wyþowten hast,
That mowthe & herte a-corden I[2]-fere,
ȝef thow wole that god þe here.

and eschew lies and oaths,

Of honde & mowþe þou moste be trewe,
And grete oþes thow moste enchewe,[3] (*sic*)
In worde and dede þou moste be mylde,
Bothe to mon and to chylde.

drunkenness, gluttony, pride, sloth, and envy.

Dronkelec[4] and glotonye,
Pruyde and slouþe and enuye,
Alle þow moste putten a-way,
ȝef þow wolt s*er*ue god to pay.
That þe nedeth, ete and drynke,
But sle þy lust for any thyng*e*.

They must keep from taverns, trading, wrestling, shooting, and the like.

Tau*er*neſ also thow moste for-sake,
And marchau*n*dyse þow schalt not make,
Wrastelyng*e*, & schotyng*e*, & suche man*er* game,
Thow myȝte not vse wythowte blame.

[Fol. 127 back.]

Hawkyng*e*, huntyng*e*,[5] and dawnsyng*e*,
Thow moste forgo for any thyng*e*;

Cutted clothes, piked shoon, markets, and fairs to be avoided.

Cuttede clothes and pyked*e* schone,
Thy gode fame þey wole for-done.
Marketes and feyres I the for-bede,
But hyt be for the more nede,
In honeste clothes[6] thow moste gon,

Armour not to be worn; beard and crown to be shaven.

Baselard*e* ny bawdryke were þow non.
Berde & crowne thow moste be schaue,
ȝef thow wole thy ordere saue.

They must practise hospitality,

Of mete and drynke þow moste be fre,
To pore and ryche by thy degre.

read the psalter, and take heed of domesday.

ȝerne[7] thow moste thy sawtere rede,
And of the day of dome haue drede;
And euer*e* do gode a-ȝeynes euele,
Or elles thow myȝte not lyue wele.

[1] ffirst. [2] in. [3] eschewe. [4] Dronkelewe.
[5] Hawkes, houndes. [6] clothing. [7] Besely.

Wy*m*mones s*er*ues [1] thow moste forsake,
Of euele fame leste they the make,
For wy*m*menes speche that ben schrewes,
Turne ofte a-way gode thewes.
  From nyse iapes [2] and rybawdye,
Thow moste turne a-way þyn ye;
Tuynde [3] þyn ye þat thow ne se
The [4] cursede worldes vanyte.
Thus thys worlde þow moste despyse,
And holy vertues haue in vyse,
Ȝef thow do þus thow schalt be dere
To alle men that sen and here.

Priests should beware of women, and especially of shrews, and avoid japes and ribaldry, that they may despise the world and follow after virtue.

Quid & quomodo predicare debet parochianos suos.

Thus thow moste also preche,
  And thy paresche ȝerne teche;
Whenne on hath done a synne,
Loke he lye not longe there-ynne,
But a-non that he hym schryue,
Be hyt [5] husbande, be hyt [6] wyue,
Leste he forȝet by lentenes day, [7]
And oute of mynde hyt go away.
  Wymmen that ben wyth chy[l]de also,
Thow moste hem teche how þey schule do.
Whe*n*ne here tyme ys negh*e* y-come,
Bydde hem do thus alle & some:
Theche hem to come & schryue hem clene,
And also hosele hem bothe at ene,
For drede of perele that may be-falle,
In here t*ra*uelyng*e* that come schalle.
To folowe the chylde ȝef hyt be nede,
Ȝef heo se hyt be in drede;
And teche the mydewyf neu*er* the latere,
That heo haue redy clene watere,

What a priest must teach his flock.

Shriving.

Women with child to go to confession,

[Fol. 128.]

and receive holy communion.

The midwife's duties.

[1] felaship. [2] gaudees. [3] Turne. [4] This. [5] he. [6] she. [7] ester day.

Thenne bydde hyre spare for no schame,
To folowe the chylde there at hame,

The child to be baptised if but half born.

And thagh*e* þe chylde bote half be bore
Hed and necke and no more,
Bydde hyre spare, neu*er* þe later,
To crystene hyt and caste on water;
And but scho mowe se þe hed,
Loke scho folowe hyt for no red;
And ȝef the wo*m*mon thenne dye,

The midwife to rip up the mother to save the child's life.

Teche the mydwyf that scho hye
For to vndo hyre wyth a knyf,
And for to saue the chyldes lyf,
And hye that hyt crystened be,
For that ys a dede of charyte.
And ȝef hyre herte ther-to grylle,

If the midwife's heart fail her she is to call in a man to help her,

Rather þenne the chylde scholde spylle,
Teche hyre thenne to calle a mon
That in that nede helpe hyre con.

for if the child is lost through her fault she may weep for it evermore.

For ȝef the chylde be so y-lore,
Scho may that wepen eu*er* more.
Bote ȝef the chylde y-bore be,
And in perele thow hyt se,
Ryght as he byd hyre done,
Caste on water and folowe hyt sone.
A-noþere way þow myght do ȝet,
In a vessel to crystone hyt;
And when scho hath do ryȝt so,

The water and vessel used in baptism to be burnt or cast into the church font.

Wat*er*e and vessel, brenne hem bo,
Othere brynge hyt to þe chyrche a-non,[1]
And caste hyt in the font ston,[1]

Baptism not to be administered twice.

But folowe thow not þe chylde twye,
Lest afterwarde hyt do the nuye.

[Fol. 128 back.]

Teche hem alle to be war and snel
That they conn*e* sey þe wordes wel,

[1] These two lines are not in Douce MS. 103.

And say the wordes alle on rowe
As a-non I wole ȝow schowe;
Say ryȝt thus and no more,
For none othere wymmenes[1] lore;

The form of baptism

¶ I folowe the, or elles[2] I crystene þe, in the nome of the fader & þe sone and the holy gost. Amen.[2]
Or elles thus,[2] Ego baptiȝo te. N. In nomine patris & filij & spiritus sancti. Amen.

may be said in English or Latin.

Englysch or latyn, whether me seyþ,
Hyt suffyseth to the feyth,
So that þe wordes be seyde on rowe,
Ryȝt as be-fore I dyde ȝow schowe;[3]
And ȝef þe cas be-falle so,

The parents may christen the child if no one else be nigh.

Þat men & wymmen be fer hyre fro,
Then may the fader wyþoute blame
Crysten the chylde and ȝeue hyt name;
So may the moder in suche a drede,
Ȝef scho se that hyt be nede.
Ȝet thow moste teche hem more,
That alle þe chyldren þat ben I-bore

Children to be christened at Easter and Whitsuntide only, except of necessity.

Byfore aster and whyssone tyde,
Eghte dayes they schullen a-byde,
That at the font halowynge
They mowe take here folowynge,
Saue tho that mowe not a-byde
For peryle of deth to that tyde.
A-nother tyme gyf hem folghthe
As the fader & þe moder wolþe.[4]

God-parents to teach their god-children pater-noster, ave, and creed,

Godfader and godmoder þou moste preche
Þat þey here godchyldere to gode teche,
Here pater noster and here crede
Techen hem they mote nede.

and not to sleep with them while very young.

By hem also they schule not slepe
Tyl þey con hem self wel kepe.

[1] kynnes. [2] Not in Douce 103. [3] myghtest knowe. [4] þoȝte.

Also wyth-ynne the fyfþe ȝere

Confirmation.

Do þat they I-bysbede were;
For tho þat bydeth ouer more,
The fader & þe moder mote rewe hyt sore;
Out of chyrche schule be put
Tyl þe byschope haue bysbede hyt.

[Fol. 129.]

And ȝet moste thow teche hem more,
That godfader and godmoder be war be-fore,

God-parents not to hold their god-children at confirmation.

¶ That they þat ben at the folowyng*e*,
Holde not þe chylde at the confermyng*e*;[1]

Relatives in blood by marriage or spiritually not to intermarry.

And also þow moste, as þ*o*u dost preche,
The cosynage of folowyng*e* teche;
And þow wolt that conne wel,
Take gode hede on thys spel.
In the myddel the chylde stont,
As he ys folowed in the font.
¶ Alle these be cosynes to hym for ay,
That none of hem he wedde may;

Who are cousins by baptism.

The p*re*ste þat foloweþ, þe p*re*stes chyldere, þe p*re*ste,
And the chyldes fader & moder, þe godfader & hys
Wyf knowe be-fore folghthe, þe godfader chylderen,
the chyldes moder and hys godfader, &c.
¶ The same cosynage in alle thyng*e*,
Is in the chyldes confermyng*e*

Who by confirmation.

The chylde þat ys confermet,[2] þe byschop, þe byschopes chylderen, þe byschop and þe chyldes fader and hys moder, the godfader and hys wyf, the chyldes fader and hys godfader, the chyldes moder and hys godmoder,
These schule neuer on wedde oþer,
But cosynes beth, as suster & broþer.
Ȝet teche hem a-nother thyng*e*,

Espousals.

That ys a poynt of weddyng*e*;
He that wole chese hym a fere,
And seyth to hyre on thys manere,

[1] bisshoping. [2] Not in Douce 103.

He who formally betroths himself to a woman must wed her.

"Here I take the to my wedded wyf,
And there-to I plyghte þe my trowþe
Wyth-owten cowpulle or fleschly dede,"
He þat wommon mote wedde nede;

His troth acts as a divorce from other women.

For þaghe he or ho a-nother take,
That word wole deuors[1] make.

Irregular marriages are cursed.

Loke also þey make non odde[2] weddynge,
Lest alle ben cursed in that doynge.
Preste & clerke and other also,
That thylke serues huydeth so;
But do ryȝt as seyn the lawes,

Banns to be asked.

Aske the banns thre halydawes.

[Fol. 129 back.]

Then lete hem come and wytnes brynge
To stonde by at here weddynge;
So openlyche at the chyrche dore
Lete hem eyther wedde othere.

Lechery a deadly sin,

Of lechery telle hem ryght þys
That dedly synne for sothe hyt ys;
On what skynnes maner so hyt be wroȝt,
Dedly synne hyt ys forthe broght,

save in wedlock.

Saue in here wedhode[3]
That ys feyre to-fore gode.
Thaȝ mon & wommon be sengul boþe,
As dedly synne they schulen hyt loþe.

Children not to sleep together after seven years of age.

Also thys mote ben hem sayde,
Boþe for knaue chyldere & for mayde,
That whenne þey passe seuen ȝere,
They schule no lengere lygge I-fere,
Leste they by-twynne hem brede
The lykynge of that fowle dede.
Also wryten wel .I. fynde,
That of synne aȝeynes kynde

Pæderastia.

Thow schalt thy paresch no þynge teche,
Ny of that synne no thynge preche;

[1] a dome. [2] hond. [3] wededhod.

Adultery is a great sin,

But say þus by gode a-vys,
Þat 'to gret synne forsoþe hyt ys,
For any mon þat bereth lyf
To forsake hys wedded wyf
And do hys kynde other way,
Þat ys gret synne wyþowte nay;'

which a man must confess to his shrift-father.

But how and where he doth þat synne,
To hys schryffader[1] he mote þat mynne.
Also thow moste thy god pay,
Teche thy paresch þus & say,
Alle that ben of warde[2] & elde
Þat cunnen hem self kepe & welde,

Confession.

They schulen alle to chyrche come,
And ben I-schryue alle & some,

Communion to be received.

And be I-hoseled wyth-owte bere
On aster day alle I-fere:
In þat day by costome
Ȝe schule be hoselet alle & some.

[Fol. 130.]

The real presence to be believed in.

Teche hem þenne wyth gode entent,
To be-leue on that sacrament;
That þey receyue in forme of bred,
Hyt ys goddes body þat soffered ded
Vp on the holy rode tre,
To bye owre synnes & make vs fre.

It is but wine and water that is given to the people after communion.

Teche hem þenne, neuer þe later,
Þat in þe chalys ys but wyn & water
That þey receyueth for to drynke
After that holy hoselynge;

Directions for receiving communion.

Therfore warne hem þow schal
That þey ne chewe þat ost to smal,
Leste to smale þey done hyt breke,
And in here teth hyt do steke;

Wine and water to be drunk after the host is eaten.

There-fore þey schule wyth water & wyn
Clanse here mowþ, that noȝt leue þer-In;

[1] confessour. [2] wytte.

But teche hem alle to leue sadde,
Þat hyt þat ys in þe awter made,
Hyt ys verre goddes blode
That he schedde on þe rode.

The consecrated wine is God's blood that was shed on the rood.

Ȝet þow moste teche hem mare
Þat whe*n*ne þey doth to chyrche fare,
Þenne bydde hem leue here mony wordes,
Here ydel speche, and nyce bordes,
And put a-way alle vanyte,
And say here pat*er* nost*er* & here aue.[1]
No non in chyrche stonde schal,
Ny lene to pyler ny to wal,
But fayre on kneus þey schule hem sette,
Knelyng*e* dou*n* vp on the flette,
And pray to god wyth herte meke
To ȝeue hem grace and m*er*cy eke.
Soffere hem to make no bere,
But ay to be in here prayere,
And whenne þe gospell*e* I-red be schalle,
Teche hem þenne to stonde vp alle,
And blesse[2] feyre as þey conne
Whenne gloria t*ib*i ys by-gonne,
And whenne þe gospel ys I-done,
Teche hem eft to knele downe sone;
And whenne they here the belle rynge
To that holy sakerynge,
Teche hem knele downe, boþe ȝonge & olde,
And boþe here hondes vp to holde,
And say þenne in þys manere,
Feyre and softely, wyth-owte bere,
"Ih*es*u, lord, welcome þow be,
In forme of bred as I þe se;
Ih*es*u! for thy holy name,
Schelde me to day fro synne & schame;

How to behave in church.

Men should there put away all vanity and say the *pater noster* and *ave.*

Not to loll about, but to kneel on the floor.

When the Gospel is read all people are to stand up.

[Fol. 130 back.]
They are to kneel when they hear the bell ring at the consecration.

A Prayer.

[1] crede.

[2] *add* hem.

Schryfte & howsele, lord,[1] þou graunte me bo,
Er that I schale hennes go,
And verre contrycyone of my synne,
That I, lord, neuer dye there-Inne;
And as þow were of a may I-bore,
Sofere me neuer to be for-lore,
But whenne þat I schale hennes wende,
Grawnte me þe blysse wyth-owten ende. AMEN."
Teche hem þus, oþer sum oþere þynge,
To say at the holy sakerynge.

All men are to kneel when they see a priest bearing the host.

Teche hem also, I the pray,
That whenne þey walken in þe way
And sene þe preste a-gayn hem comynge,
Goddes body wyth hym berynge,
Thenne, wyth grete deuocyone,
Teche hem þere to knele a-downe;
Fayre ne fowle, spare þey noghte
To worschype hym þat alle hath wroghte;

The benefits received by seeing the host, according to St. Augustinus.

For, glad[2] may þat mon be
þat ones in þe day may hym se;
For so mykyle gode doþ þat syȝt,
(As seynt austyn techeth a-ryȝt,)
þat day þat þow syst goddes body,
þese benefyces schalt þou haue sycurly;[3]

The recipient on that day shall not lack food, shall be forgiven idle words and oaths, shall not [Fol. 131.] fall by sudden death, nor become blind.

Mete & drynke at thy nede,
Non schal þe þat day be-gnede;[4]
Idele othes and wordes also
God for-ȝeueþ the bo;
Soden deth that ylke day,
The dar not drede wyþowte nay;
Also þat[5] day I the plyȝte
þow schalt not lese þyn ye syȝte;

[1] *lord* must be a later insertion, as it makes the line 5 feet.
[2] Two emphatic syllables for 2 feet.
[3] Douce 103 gives this line thus:—"Thou shalt haue þes sikerly."
[4] grede. [5] thilk.

And eu*er*y fote þ*at* þou gost þenne,
þ*at* holy syȝt for to sene,
þey schule be tolde to stonde in stede
Whenne thow hast to hem nede.

Games not to be played in church or churchyard.

Also wyth-ynne chyrche & seyntwary[1]
Do ryȝt thus as I the say,
Song*e* and cry[2] and suche fare,
For to stynte þow schalt not spare;
Castyng*e* of axtre & eke of ston,
Sofere hem þere to vse non;
Bal and bares and suche play,
Out of chyrcheȝorde put a-way;

Courts not to be held there.

Courte-holdyng*e* and suche man*er* chost,
Out of seyntwary[3] put þow most;
For cryst hym self techeth vs

The church God's house.

þ*at* holy chyrche ys hys hows,
þ*at* ys made for no þyng*e* elles[4]
But for to p*ra*ye In, as þe boke telles;[5]
þere þe pepull*e* schale geder w*ith* Inne
To p*ra*yen and to wepen for here synne.

Tythes to be duly paid,

Teche hem also well*e* and greythe
How þey schule paye here teythe:
Of alle þyng*e* that doth hem newe,
They schule teythe well*e* & trewe,
After þe costome of þat cuntraye
Eu*er*y mon hys teythyng*e*[6] schale paye

of small things and great, sheep, swine, and other live cattle.

Bothe of smale and of grete,
Of schep and swyn & oþer nete.
Teyþe of huyre and of honde,
Goth by costome of þe londe.

[1] chirch hay.

[2] There is a note in Douce 103, *f.* 126*b*, in a hand a few years later than the text:—"Da*n*seyng, cotteyng, bollyng, tenessy*n*g, hand ball, fott ball, stoil ball & all mann*er* other gam*es* out cherc*h*yard.

I ye pra & reyng þ*at* lent no be ther
As it were in merket or fair."

[3] churchyerd. [4] moȝt elles. [5] bookes. [6] Eche one teythe.

It is useless to speak much of tithing, even ignorant priests understand that.

I holde hyt but an ydul þynge
To speke myche of teythynge,
For þaȝ a preste be but a fonne,[1]
Aske hys teyþynge, welle he conne.[2]

Witchcraft forbidden.

Wychecrafte and telynge,
Forbede þou hem for any þynge;

[Fol. 131 back.]

For who so be-leueth in þe fay
Mote be-leue thus by any way,
That hyt ys a sleghþe of þe del[3]
Þat makeþ a body to cache el.[4]
Þenne syche be-leue he gart hem haue,
Þat wychecrafte schale hem saue,
So wyth chames[5] & wyth tele,
He ys I-broȝte aȝeyn to hele.
Þus wyth þe fende he ys I-blende,
And hys by-leue ys I-schende.

Usury forbidden.

Vsure and okere þat beth al on,
Teche hem þat þey vse non;
That ys a synne fulle greuus
By-fore owre lord swete Ihesus.
God taketh myche on gref

Men not to sell at too high a price.

To selle a mon in hys myschef
Any þynge to hye prys.
For welle he wot þat oker hyt ys,
And lene .xij d. to haue .xiij.
For þat [is] vsure wyþowte wene.
Teche hem also to lete one,
To selle þe derrer for þe lone.

To preche hem also þou myȝt not wonde,—
Bothe to wyf and eke husbonde,—

Husbands and wives not to make vows of chastity,

Þat nowþer of hem no penaunce take,
Ny non a-vow to chastite make,

[1] fon. [2] kon.
[3] Or 'de[ue]l,' like Shakspere's 'deale,' and 'eale'=evil—in Hamlet, 202, and Scotch 'deil.' Cf. ȝen = given, 25/795, and 'sene'=seven in other texts.
[4] Or 'e[ue]l.' [5] charmes: chames in the text is probably a scribal error.

Ny no pylg*r*image take to do,
But ȝef boþe assente þer to.
These þre poyntes verement
Nowþ*er* schale do, but boþe assent,

penance, or pilgrimage without the consent of each other.

Saue þe vow [1] to Iherusalem,
Þat ys lawful to eþ*er* of hem.
Þenne schale þe husbonde als blyue [2]
Teche & p*re*che so hys wyue,

Except the vow of a pilgrimage to Jerusalem.

That heo a-vow no man*er* þyng*e*
But hyt be at hys wytyng*e*;
For þaȝ heo do, hyt may not stonde
But heo haue grawu*n*te of hyre husbonde;

Wives not to make vows unknown to their husbands.

And ȝef þe husbonde assente þer-to,
Þenne nedely hyt mote be do;
No more schale he verement,
But hys wyf þ*er*to assent.

[Fol. 132.]

The pater noster and þe crede,
Preche þy paresch*e* þ*o*u moste nede,
Twyes or þryes in þe ȝere
To þy paresch hole and fere;

Pater noster and creed to be taught.

Teche hem þus, and byd hem say
Wyþ gode entent eu*er*y day,
"FAder owre þat art in heuene,
Halowed be þy name wi*th* meke steuene,

The "Our Father."

Þy kyngdom be for to come
In vs s*y*nfull*e* alle and some;
Þy wylle be do in erþe here
As hyt ys in heuene clere;
Owre vche dayes bred, we þe pray,
Þat þow ȝeue vs þys same day;
And forgyue vs owre trespas
As we done hem þ*at* gult vs has;
And lede vs in-to no fondyng*e*,
But schelde vs alle from euel þyng*e*. Amen."

[1] avoue. [2] to stynt stryfe.

The "Hail, Mary."

"HAyl be þow, mary, fulle of grace;
God ys wyþ þe in euery[1] place;
I-blessed be þow of alle wymmen,
And þe fruyt of þy wombe Ihesus![2] Amen!"

The "I believe."

"I be-leue in oure holy dryȝt,
Fader of heuene, god almyȝt,
þat alle thynge has wroȝt,
Heuene and erþe & alle of noȝt:
On ihesu cryst I be-leue also,
Hys only sone, and no mo,
þat was conceyuede of þe holy spyryt,
And of a mayde I-bore quyt,
And afterward vnder pounce pylate
Was I-take for vye and hate,
And soffrede peyne and passyone,
And on þe croys was I-done;

[Fol. 132 back.]

Ded and buryed he was also,
And wente to helle to spoyle oure fo,
And ros to lyue the þryde day,
And stegh to heuene þe .xl. day[3]:
ȝet he schale come wyþ woundes rede
To deme þe quyke and þe dede.
In þe holy gost I leue welle;
In holy chyrche and hyre spelle.
In goddes body I be-leue nowe,
A-monge hys seyntes to ȝeue me rowe;
And of my synnes þat I haue done,
To haue plenere remyssyone,
And when my body from deth schal ryse,
I leue to be wyth god and hyse,
And haue the ioye þat lasteþ ay;
God graunte hym self þat I so may! Amen!"

[1] eche a.   [2] MS. Ihc.   [3] what tyme he say.

The Articles of Faith.

The artykeles of the fey
Teche þy paresch þus, & sey ;
That seuene[1] to dyuynyte,
And .vij. to the humanyte.

1. Believe on Father, Son, and Holy Ghost.

¶ *Primus.* The fyrste artykele ys (þou wost)
Leue on fader and sone & holy gost.

2. The Father is God Almighty.

¶ ij*us*. The secou*n*de ys to leue ryȝt
þat þe fader ys god al myȝt.

3. Jesus Christ is the Son of God,

¶ iij*us*. The þrydde ys, as þow syst,
For to leue on ihesu cryst,
þat he ys goddes sone ryȝt,
And boþe on god & of on myȝt.

and one with him.

4. The Holy Ghost is God,

¶ iiij*us*. The holy gost, persone þrydde,
Leueth also, I ȝow bydde,
That he ys god wyth oþ*er* two,
And ȝet on god and no mo.

and one with Father and Son.

Leste þys be hard*e* ȝow to leue,
By ensau*m*pul I wole þat preue :
Se þe ensau*m*pul þ*at* I ȝow schowe,
Of water and ys and eke snowe ;
Here beth þre þynges, as ȝe may se,
And ȝet þe þre, alle water be.

An illustration: water, ice, and snow are three and yet one.

Thus þe fader and þe sone & þe holy gost
Beth on god of myȝtes most ;
For þagh þey be person*us* þre,
In on godhed knyt they be.

[Fol. 133.]

Thus it is with the Father, Son, and Holy Ghost.

5. Who have made with one assent heaven, earth, and hell.

¶ v*us*. These þre in on godhede,
Wyth on assent and on rede,
Alle þyng*e* made wyth on spelle,
Heuene, and vrþe, and eke helle.

6. Power of the Holy Ghost.

¶ vj. The sexþe artykele, ȝef ȝe wole fynde,
Holy chyrche taketh in mynde
That þorȝ þe myȝt of þe holy gost
Is in vrthe of power most,

3

[1] *add* pe*r*teyneth.

And as myȝty, as I ȝow telle,
Boþe of þe ȝates of heuene & helle
To tuynen and open at heyre byddynge
Wythowte ȝeyn-stondynge of any þynge.

7. The Resurrection.

¶ vijus. The seuenþe artykele, for soþe hyt ys,
þat he schal ende in ioye & blys
When body and soule to-geder schal come,
And the gode to ioye be I-nome,
And the euel be put a-way
In-to the peyne that lasteþ ay.

8. Jesus Christ became man in Mary's womb.

¶ viijus. The eghþe artykele ys not to hele,
þe strengþe of oure feyth þe more dele,
The flesch and blod þat ihesus tok
In mayde mary, as seyth þe bok,
þorȝ the holy gostes myȝt
þat in þat holy vyrgyne lyȝt.

9. Who was a Virgin.

¶ ixus. The nynþe artykele ys for to mene
þat he was bore of a mayde clene.

10. The Lord's passion.

¶ xus. þe tenþe artykele oure synne sleth,
Crystes passyone and hys deth.

11. He went down into Hell, in soul and Godhead, while his body was in the tomb.

¶ xjus. The eleuenþe ys for to telle
How he wente to spoyle helle,
In soule and godhede wyth-owte nay
Whyle the body in towmbe lay.

12. He rose again.

¶ xijus. The twelfþe artykele makeþ vs fayn,
For he ros to lyue a-gayn
The þrydde day in the morowe,
For to bete alle oure sorowe.

[Fol. 133 back.]

13. He went up into Heaven on Holy Thursday.

¶ xiijus. The þreteneþe artykele, as telle I may,
þat cryst hym self on holy þursday
Stegh in-to heuene in flesch & blode,
That dyede by-forn[1] on þe rode.

14. He shall come again at Domesday to judge the

¶ xiiijus. The fourteneþ artykele, ys soþe to say,
þat cryst schale come on domes day

[1] bifor.

Wyþ hys wou*n*des fresch and rede
To deme þe quyke and þe dede.
Here ben þe artykeles of þe fey;
Preche[1] hem ofte I þe prey.

living and the dead.

¶ Septem sacramenta ecclesie.

The Seven Sacraments.

TO p*re*che also þow myȝt not[2] yrke
þe .vij. sacramentes of holy chyrche.[3]
þat ys folghþe þat clanseþ synne,
And confermyng*e* aft*er*, as we may mynne,[4]
The sacrament of goddes body,
And also penau*n*ce þat ys verrey,
Ordere of p*re*st, and spousayle,
And þe laste elyng*e* wyth-owte fayle;
Lo here the seuene and no mo,
Loke thow preche ofte þo.

I. Baptism.
II. Confirmation.
III. The Eucharist.
IV. Penance.
V. VI. Orders and Matrimony.
VII. Unction.

¶ De sacramento baptismatis.

Baptism.

ȝEt I mote in thys worchyng*e*
Teche the more of folowyng*e*,
For hyt ys syche a sacrament
þat may lyȝtely be I-schent
But hyt be done redyly
In vche[5] a poynte by and by;
Therfore do as I the say,
Lest thow go out of þe way.
Hast þou wel vnderstonde my lore
As I taghte the by-fore,
How þou schuldest wy*m*men lere
þ*at* wyth chylde grete were?
But þys ys for þyn owne prow
þat I here teche the now.
ȝef a chylde myscheueth at home,
And ys I-folowed & has hys[6] nome,

Children baptized at home to be brought to church.

[1] Teche. [2] die. [3] kirk. [4] nym. [5] eu*er*y. [6] no.

[Fol. 134.]

ȝef hyt to chyrche be broȝt to þe
As hyt oweth for to be,
Thenne moste þou slyly [1]

The priest to ask those present at the baptism whether the words were said aright.

Aske of hem þat were þere by,
How þey deden þen in þat cas
Whenne þe chylde I-folowede was,
And wheþer þe wordes were seyde a-ryȝt,
And not turnet in þat hyȝt;
ȝef þe wordes were seyde on rowe
As lo here I do þe schowe,

Ista sunt uerba baptismi In domo.

The words of baptism.

¶ I crystene þe, or elles I folowe þe, .N. In nome of þe fader and the sone, and the holy gost. Amen.

And þagh þou ȝeue no name to hem,
Ny nempne hem no maner name,
I telle hyt for no blame,
Hyt may be don al by thoght
Whenne hyt ys to chyrche I-broght,
And þaȝ me say, as þey done vse,
Sory laten in here wyse, As þus,

Bad Latin spoils not the Sacrament,

I folowe þe in nomina patria & filia spiritus sanctia.
AmeN.
Of these wordes take þow non hede,
Þe folghþe ys gode wythoute drede
So þat here entent & here wyt
Were forto folowe hyt;

if the first syllable of each word be right.

Ay whyle þey holde þe fyrste sylabul,
Þe folghþe ys gode wythouten fabul, As þus,
Pa of patris. fi of filij. spi of spiritus sancti. Amen.
Þenne do þe seruyse neuer þe later,
Alle saue þe halowynge of þe water;

Holy oil to be used.

Creme & crysme and alle þynge elles
Do to þe chylde as þe bok telles;

[1] full sotelly.

And ȝef þe chylde haue nome by-fore,
Lete hyt stonde in goddes ore;
And ȝef hyt haue not, lete name hyt þare,
Ȝef hyt schule in greyþe fare.
 But what and on in hys bordes
Caste on water and say þe wordes,
Is þe chylde I-folowed or no?
By god, I say nay for hem bo,
But ȝef hyt were hys full*e* entent
To ȝeue þe chylde þat sac*ra*ment,
Þenne mote hyt stonde wyþoute nay, As þus,
And he þerfore rewe hyt may.
¶ But ȝef cas falle thus,
Þat he þe wordes sayde a-mys,
Or þus In no*mine* filij & p*at*ris & sp*iritus* s*ancti*. Amen.
Or any oþer wey but þey set hem on rowe,
As þe fader & þe sone & þe holy gost,
In no*mine* p*at*ris & filij & sp*iritus* s*ancti*. Amen.
Ȝef hyt be oþ*er* weyes .I.-went,
Alle þe folghþe ys clene I-schent;
Þenne moste þou, to make hyt trewe,
Say þe serues all*e* a-newe,
Blesse þe water & halowe þe font,
Ryght as hyt in bok stont;
Þenne be þe war in alle þyng*e*,
Whenne þou comest to þe plungyng*e*,
Þenne þou moste say ryȝt þus,
Or elles þou dost alle a-mys,
¶ Si tu es baptiȝat*us*, ego te no*n* rebaptiȝo. S*ed* si non es baptiȝat*us*, ego te baptiȝo. In no*mine* p*at*ris & filij & sp*iritus* s*ancti*. amen.
Þat oþer serues say þow myȝt
On þy bok all*e* forth ryght;
Þow moste do þe same manere
Ȝef a chylde I-fownde were,

[Fol. 134 back.] If a person uses the matter and form of baptism in jest, it is not a sacrament unless he intended it to be so.

If the words are said in wrong order the sacrament is nought.

When the baptism has not been valid, the priest is to perform the holy rite over again,

and say thus.

Form of conditional baptism.

A foundling is to be conditionally baptized.

And no mon cowþe telle þere
Wheþer hyt were folowed or hyt nere;
þenne do to hyt in alle degre,
As here before þou myȝt se.

If a priest be so drunken that his tongue serves him not he must not baptize.

But what & þou so dronken be
þat þy tonge wole not serue þe,
þenne folowe þow not by no way
But þou mowe the wordes say.

[Fol. 135.]

Luytel I-noghe for-soþe hyt ys,
Thaghe thow be bothe war & wys,
The sacrament for to do,
Thaghe þou pe neuer so abul þer to;
How schulde þenne a droken[1] mon
Do þat þe sobere vnneþe con?

Oil and creme to be always in readiness.

And ȝef þow wole þy worschype saue,
Oyle & creme þow moste nede haue,
Alway redy for ferde of drede,
To take þer-to when þou hast nede.

Creme to be changed yearly.

And for to eschewe þe byschopus scheme,
Vche ȝere ones chawnge þy creme,
And þat as sone as thow may,

After Holy Thursday the oil to be changed.

A-non after schere þursday,
Thow moste chawnge þyn oyle also,
þat þey mowe be newed bo.

Confirmation.

ȝet wole I make relacyone
To þe of confyrmacyone,
þat in lewde[2] mennes menynge
Is I-called þe byspynge;
But for þow hast þer-of luytel to done,
þer-fore I lete hyt passe ouer sone,
For hyt ys þe bisschopes ofyce,
I wot þe charge ys alle[3] hyse,
But ȝet I wole seche ȝerne
Sumwhat þer-of to make þe lerne.

[1] dronken. [2] by englisshe. [3] also.

must be performed by a bishop.

þat sacrament mote nede be done,
Of a bysschope nede as ston;
þer nys no mon of lower degre,
þat may þat do, but onlyche he:

No man of lower degree can perform it.

He confermeth, & maketh sad,
þat at þe preste be-forn hath mad;
Wherfore þe nome þat ys þenne I-spoke
Moste stonde ferme as hyt were loke[1];

The name given in confirmation not to be changed.

But ofte syþes þou hast I-sen
Whenne þe chyldre confermed ben
Bondes a-bowte here neckes be lafte,
þat from hem schule not be rafte,
Tyl at chyrche þe eghþe[2] day,
þe preste hym self take hem a-way.

The bonds to be left about the necks of children who have been confirmed until the eighth day.

[Fol. 135 back.]

þenne schale he wyth hys owne hondes
Brenne þat ylke same bondes,
And wassche þe chylde ouer þe font
þere he was anoynted in þe front.
And þagh a chylde confermet nere,
So þat he folowed by-fore were,
To dyspuyte þer-of hyt ys no nede,
He schale be saf wythowte drede.

The child to be washed over the front on the eighth day.

De modo audiendi confessionem.

NOw y praye þe take gode hede,
For þys þou moste conne nede,
Of schryfte & penaunce I wole þe telle,
And a whyle þere-In dwelle;

Confession and penance.

But myche more þou moste wyten,
þenne þou fyndest here I-wryten,
And whenne þe fayleþ þer to wyt,
Pray to god to sende þe hyt,
For ofte þou moste penaunce ȝen
Boþe to men and to wymmen,

The shrift-father must know much more than is told here. He is to pray to God for wit.

[1] stoke. [2] vij.

Oþer weyes þen wole þe lawe
Leste they token hyt to harde on awe,

Legal penances are very hard, and must be given discreetly.

Hyt were fulle harde þat penaunce to do
That þe lawes ordeyneth to,
Therfore by gode dyscrecyone,
Þow moste in confessyone,
Ioyne penaunce bothe harde & lyȝte,
As þou here aftere lerne myȝte.

Penance without shrift helps little the soul.

But sykerly penaunce wyþowte schryfte[1]
Helpeþ luytel þe sowle þryfte;[1]
Þerfore of schryfte I wole þe kenne
And to ioyne penaunce þenne,
To here schryft þou moste be fayn,
And hye þerto wythowte layn.

When a man goes to confession he is to kneel, and the priest is to ask him if he be of his parish.

And fyrst, when any mon I-schryue wole be,
Teche hym to knele downe on hys kne;
Fyrst þow moste aske hym þen,
Wheþer he be þy paresschen;

[Fol. 136.]

If he be not, the priest may not hear his shrift unless he had leave to come from his own parish priest.

And ȝef he vnswere and say nay,
Theche hym home fayre hys way,
But he schowe þe I-wryten,
Where-by þou myȝt wel I-wyten,
Þat he hath leue of hys prest
To be I-schryue where hym lust,

A man may leave his parish priest and go to confession elsewhere for these reasons:—

For these poyntes wyþowte nay
He may haue leue to go hys way,
And schryue hym at a noþer prest
Where that hym beste lust,[2]

If his parish priest be indiscreet;

Leste indyscrete hys prest were,
Hys confessyone for to here,

if he knew that his confession would be revealed;

Or ȝef he knewe by redy token
Þat hys schryfte he wolde open,

if he had done a sin with any of the priest's near

Or ȝef hym self had done a synne
By þe prestes sybbe kynne,

[1] These two lines are not in Douce 103.
[2] The foregoing five lines are not in Douce 103.

Moder, or suster, or hys le*m*mon,
Or by hys doghter ȝef he hade on,

kindred, as mother, sister, concubine, or daughter;

Or ȝef he stonde hym on awe,
To dedly synne leste he hym drawe,

if he feared that his priest would draw him into sin;

Or ȝef he hade vndertake
Any pylgrymage for to make,

if he had made a vow of pilgrimage;

Or ȝef hys prest (as doctor*us* sayn)
By any of hys paresch haue layn,

or if the priest had lain with any of his parishioners.

For þese he may leue take,
And to a-noþer hys schryfte make,
And werne hym leue hys p*re*st ne may
Lest hyt greue hym a-noþer day;
And þaȝ he do, for noȝt hyt ys,
Þe byschope wole ȝeue hy*m* leue I-wys.

Of scoler, of flotterer, or of passyngere
Here schryft lawfully þ*o*u myȝt here;

A priest may hear the confession of a scholar, a sailor, or a passenger;

And also in a-noþer cas,
Ȝef þ*o*u a mon a-corset has,
He mote nede be soyled of þe,
Whoso pareschen eu*er* he be;

and if he has cursed any one he must absolve him.

And of mon þat schal go fyȝte
In a bateyl for hys ryȝte,
Hys schryft also þ*o*u myȝte here,
Þaȝ he þy p*ar*eschen neuer were;

He may also hear the shrift of a person about to go to battle;

[Fol. 136 back.]

And of a mon þat deth ys negh:
Here hys schryft, but þen be slegh,

or of one near death, though he be not a parishioner.

Byd hym & oþ*er* also by-fore,
Ȝef þat þey to lyf keuere,[1]
Þat þey go for more socour
To here owne curatour,
And schryue hem newe to hym bo
And take he penau*n*ce newe also.

Penitents are to be bidden to go afterwards to their own curates and shrive them anew.

¶ Or ȝef any do a synne,
And þy paresch be wyth-Inne,

If any man sin in the parish,

[1] kore.

Of þat synne a-soyle hym þenne,
Þaȝ he be not þy pareschenne,
But ȝef þe synne be so stronge,
To þe byschope þat hyt longe,

or have an office there, his confession may be heard.

Or ȝef a mon be seruaunt,
In þy paresch by couenaunt,
Or hath an ofyce or bayly,
Þat he ledeth hys lyf by,
And hys howseholde be elles where,
Pareschen he ys þenne þere;

A person may be wedded who has plighted troth in the parish.

Or ȝef any hath trowþe I-plyȝt
Wyþ-Inne þy paresch to any wyȝt,
Þenne þou myȝt hem wedden I-fere,
As hyt ys the court[1] manere.
But to þyn owne pareschenne
Do ryȝt þus as I þe kenne,

The priest is to teach his own flock to kneel. He is then to pull his hood over his eyes.

Teche hym to knele downe on hys kne
Pore oþer ryche wheþer he be,
Þen ouer þyn yen pulle þyn hod,
And here hys schryfte wyþ mylde mod.

When a woman comes to confession he is not to look on her face,

But when a wommon cometh to þe,
Loke hyre face þat þou ne se,
But teche hyre to knele downe þe by,
And sum-what þy face from hyre þou wry,

but to sit still as a stone;

Stylle as ston þer[2] þow sytte,
And kepe þe welle þat þou ne spytte.

nor to spit or cough,

Koghe þow not þenne, þy þonkes,
Ny wrynge þou not wyth þy schonkes,

[Fol. 137.]

Lest heo suppose þow make þat fare,
For wlatynge þat þou herest þare,

but to remain still as any maid.

But syt þou stylle as any mayde
Tyl þat heo haue alle I-sayde;

When she hesitates,

And when heo stynteþ & seyþ no more,
Ȝef þou syst heo nedeth lore,

[1] D. 103, couthe.

[2] þen.

þenne spek to hyre on þys wyse,
And say, "take þe gode a-vyse,
And what man*er* þyng*e* þ*o*u art gulty of,
Telle me boldely & make no scof.
Telle me þy synne, I þe praye,
And spare þow not by no waye;
Wonde þow not for no schame,
Parauent*ur* I haue done þe same,
And fulhelt myche more,
ȝef þow knew alle my sore,
Wherfore, sone,[1] spare þow noȝt,
But telle me what ys in þy þoȝt."
 And when he seyþ 'I con no more,'
Freyne hym þus, & grope hys sore,
"Sone or doghter, now herken me,
For su*m*-what I wole helpe þe,
And when þou herest what þow hast do
Knowlache wel a-non þer to.

he is to encourage her to speak boldly,

by saying he has perhaps sinned as bad or worse.

¶ Hic incipit inquisicio in confessione.

"Const þow þy pater and þyn aue
And þy crede, now telle þow me."
ȝef he seyth he con hyt not,
Take hys penau*n*ce þenne he mot.
To suche penau*n*ce þenne þ*o*u hym t*ur*ne,
þat wole make hym hyt to lerne.

If the penitent does not know the pater, ave, and creed, he is to have such a penance set as will make him learn them.

¶ Quod sufficit scire in lingua materna.

ȝef he conne hyt in hys tonge,
To ȝeue hym penau*n*ce hyt ys wronge.
But of þe artykeles of þe fey,
þus appose hym þenne, & sey,

He is to be examined in the articles of the faith, and be asked—

[1] ? daughter.

Believest thou in Father, Son, and Holy Ghost;

"Be-leuest þow on fader & sone & holygost,
As þou art holden, wel þow wost,
Thre persons in trynyte,
And on god (vnsware þow me),

[Fol. 137 back.]

þat goddes sone monkynde toke,
In mayde mary (as seyth þe boke),
And of þat mayde was I-bore:
Leuest þow þys? telle me by-fore,

in the Incarnation;

And on crystes passyone,
And on hys resurrexyone,
And stegh vp in-to heuen blys
In flesch and blod (be-leuest þow þys?),
And schal come with woundes rede
To deme þe quyke and þe dede,
And we vch one (as we ben here)
In body and sowle bothe I-fere,
Schule ryse at þe day of dome
And be redy at hys come,
And take þenne for oure doynge,
As we haue wroȝt here lyuynge,
Who so has do wel schale go to blysse,
Who so has do euel to peyne I-wysse.
Be-leuest also verrely [1]
þat hyt ys goddes owne body,
þat þe prest ȝeueth the
Whenne þou schalt I-hoseled be?
Leuest also in fulle a-tent,
How þat holy sacrament,
Is I-ȝeue to mon kynne
In remyssyone of here synne;
Be-leuest also, now telle me,
þat he þat lyueþ in charyte
Schale come to blysse sycurly,
And dwelle in seyntes cumpany?"

on Christ's Passion and Resurrection;

and his coming to judge the quick and the dead,

when the good shall go to bliss and the bad to pain?

Believest thou that it is God's own body which the priest gives at the houseling?

[1] sadly.

Hec sunt .x. precepta dei.

The Ten Commandments.

Þe .x. cummawndementes of god almyȝt,
I wole the aske a-non ryght,
And ȝef þou haue any I-borste,
Telle me a-non þow moste.

I. Hast thou worshipped anything above God?

¶ Hast þou worschypet any þyng*e*
More þen god, oure heuene kyng*e*?

Hast thou had dealings with evil spirits, conjuring, or witchcraft, or [Fol. 138.] sorcery, or doubted any article of the faith?

Hast þow lafte goddes name,
And called þe fend in any gr*a*me?
Hast þow any tyme I-made *con*iurynge,
For þefte or for any oþer þyng*e*?
Hast þow made any wych-crafte,
For any þyng*e* þat þe was rafte?
Hast þow made any sorcery
To gete wy*m*men to lyg*e* hem by?
Hast þou had dowte, by any way,
In any poynt of the fey?

II. Hast thou taken false oaths, or sworn lightly?

¶ Seche þyn herte trewly ore
Ȝef þow were any tyme forswore,
At court or hundret or at schyre,
For loue or drede or any huyre.
Hast þou be wonet to swere als,
By goddes bones or herte, fals,
What by hys wou*n*des, nayles or tre,
Whe*n*ne þow myȝtes haue lete be?
Hast þou be wonet to swere ȝerne
For þyng*e* þat dyde to noȝt turne?
Hast þow any tyme þy trowþe I-plyȝt,
And broken hyt a-gayn þe ryȝt?

III. Hast thou kept the Holy-days, gone to church, avoided work and riotous company

¶ Hast þow holden þyn halyday,
And spend hyt wel to goddes pay?
Hast þow .I.-gon to chyrche fayn
To serue god wyþ alle þy mayn?
Hast þou any werke þ*a*t day I-wroȝt,
Or synned sore in dede or þoȝt?

Be-þenke þe wel, sone, I rede,
Of þy synne and þy mysdede.

Shooting and other sports, going to the ale on holy-days, singing and rioting, injure the soul.

For schotynge, for wrastelynge, & oþer play,
For goynge to þe ale on halyday,
For syngynge, for roytynge, & syche fare,
Þat ofte þe sowle doth myche care.[1]

Holy-days were ordained for God's service and to hear mass.

Þe halyday only ordeynet was,
To here goddes serues and þe mas,
And spene þat day in holynes,
And leue alle oþer bysynes;
For, a-pon þe werkeday,
Men be so bysy in vche way,

[Fol. 138 back.]

Men are so busy on other days that they have little time for devotion.

So that for here ocupacyone,
Þey leue myche of here deuocyone;
Þerfore þey schule here halyday
Spene only god to pay;
And ȝef þey do any oþer þynge
Þen serue god by here cunnynge,
Þen þey brekeþ goddes lay
And holdeth not here halyday.

IV. Hast thou honoured thy father and mother?

¶ Hast þow honowred by þy wyt
Fader and moder, as god þe byt?
Hast þou any tyme made hem wroth,
In word or dede þat was hem loth?

Hast thou given them meat, drink, and raiment at their need? Hast thou had prayers said for the repose of their souls?

Hast þou ȝeue hem, at here nede,
Mete & drynke, cloþ or wede?
Ȝef þey ben dede & gon here way,
Hast þow made for hem to pray?
Hast þow done also honowre
To hym þat ys þy curatowre?
Leue welle, sone, in gode lewte,
I say not þys for loue of me,
But for þow owest to do honour
To hym þat ys þy curatour.[2]

[1] D 103, That moche agen the soule are.
[2] The foregoing four lines are not in Douce 103 or 60.

V. Hast thou slain

¶ Hast þow any mon I-slayn,
Or holpe þer-to by þy mayn;
Hast þou cou*n*celed or ȝeue mede
To any mon to do þat dede?
Hast þou any mon wowndet in debate,
Or had to hym any dedly hate?

or wounded any one?

¶ Hast þou ȝeue any mon of þy mete,
When he hade hong*ur* and nede to ete?
By euel esau*m*pull*e* þow myȝt also,
A-noþer monnes sowle slo;
Þ*er*fore take hede on þy lyuyng*e*
Ȝef þou haue trespaset in syche þyng*e*.

Hast thou slain any one's soul by bad example?

¶ Hast þou in synne I-lad þy lyf,
And put a-way þyn owne wyf;
Hast þou I-do þat ylke synne
To any of þy sybbe kynne?
Take also wel in mynde,
Ȝef þou haue sched þyn owne kynde,
Slepyng*e* or wakyng*e* nyȝt or day,
In what maner þow moste say.

VI. Hast thou put away thy wife, or otherwise sinned against chastity?

[Fol. 139.]

¶ Hast þou stolen any þyng*e*,
Or ben at any robbyng*e*;
Hast þou, by maystry or by craft,
Any mon hys good be-raft?
Hast þou I-fou*n*de any þyng*e*
And helet hyt at askyng*e*?
Hast þou vset mesures fals,
Or wyghtes þ*at* were als
By þe more to bye, & by þe lasse to selle?
Ȝef þou haue so done þow moste hyt telle.
Hast þou borowet oght wel fayn,
And not I-quyt hyt wel a-gayn?
Hast þou wyth-holden any teyþyng*e*,
Or mys-I-teyþed, by þy wytyng*e*?

VII. Hast thou stolen anything, or been at a robbing; used false measures or weights; borrowed things and not returned them, or withholden tithes?

¶ Hast þow boren any wytnes
A-gayn þe ryȝt in falsnes?

VIII. Hast thou borne false witness or got anything by perjury?

Hast þow lyet any lesynge,
To greue any mon in any þynge?
Hast þou geten wyth fals swore[1]
Any þynge lasse or more?

IX. Hast thou coveted thy neighbour's goods, his house, cattle, horse, or mare?

¶ Hast þou I-coueted wyþ alle þy myȝt,
þy neghbores good, agayn þe ryȝt;
Hows[2] or catel, hors or mare,
Or oght þat he myȝt euel spare?

X. Thou sinnest ill if thou wishest for thy neighbour's wife.

¶ Also þou dost syngen ylle,
þy neghbores wyf for to wylle,
For þat, god for-bedeþ the:
ȝef þou haue done, now telle þou me.
þow myȝte synge als sore in þoght,
As þou þat dede hadest I-wroght,
ȝef þow in þy þoght haue lykynge
To do þat ylke fowle þynge.

The desire to do evil is itself a sin.

þus þow myȝte synge dedlyche
ȝef þow þenke þer-on myche.
These ben þe cummawndementes ten,
þat god ȝaf to alle men.

[Fol. 139 back.]

¶ De modo inquirendi de .vij. peccatis mortalibus.

Of deadly sins.

Of dedly synnes now also,
I wole þe aske now er þow go.
þerfore, sone, spare þow noght,
To telle how þou hast hem wroȝt.

¶ De superbia.

Hast thou, knowingly, made God angry;

HAst þou any tyme wytyngly,
I-wrathþad þy god greuowsly?
Hast þow ben inobedyent
A-gayn goddes cummawndement?

for pride despised him who has taught thee good?

Hast þou for pruyde I-set at noght
Hym þat hath þe gode I-taght?

[1] ware. [2] cowe.

Hast þou any tyme bost I-mad,
Of any good þat þou hast had
Only of þyn owne wyt,
When god hym self ȝaf þe hyt?
  Hast thow forsake þyn owne gult,
And on a-noþer þe blame I-pult?
Hast þou feynet the holy
By ypocryse and foly?
Hast þou any tyme I-feynet þe
Gode and holy on to se,
In hope on þat man*er* to huyde
Boþe þy synne and þy pruyde?
  Hast þow any tyme I-take on þe
Any gode dede of charyte
Þat was a-noþ*er* monnes doyng*e*,
And of þyn no maner þyng*e*?
  Hast þow ay opp*res*set þy neghbo*ur*
For to gete þe hono*ur*?
Hast þou I-schend hys gode fame
For to gete þe a gode name?
  Hast þou also prowde I-be
Of any vertu þat god ȝaf þe?
For þy voys was gode & hye,
Or for þy wyt was gode & slye,
Or for thy[1] her*us* were cryspe & longe,
Or for þow hast a renabull*e*[2] tonge,
[Or for thy body is fayr & long,
Or for þou art white & strong,[3]]
Or for þy flesch ys whyte and clene,
Or any syche degre to say at ene?
  Hast þou be prowde and eke of port
For tryste of lady and eke of lord?
Hast þou be prowde of worschype or gode,
Or for þow come of grete blode?

Hast thou laid the blame of thine own sin on another?

Hast thou pretended to be holy to hide sin and pride?

Hast thou passed off others' good deeds as thine own,

or oppressed thy neighbour to get honour;

or been proud of thy virtues, thy voice, thy wit, thy hair, thy body, or thy strength;

[Fol. 140.]

or that thou art trusted by lady or lord, or that thou comest of high family?

[1] thy D, hys Cl. [2] resonable. [3] Not in Cotton MS.

Hast thou been proud on account of any office that thou hast held?

Hast þou any tyme þe prodder þe mad,
For any ofyce þat þow hast had?
  Hast þow be prowde gostely,—
Telle me, sone, baldely,—
Of mekenes, of pacyens, or of pyte,
Of pouert, of largenes, or of chastyte,
And oþer vertues mony mo?
Wayte[1] lest þou haue synget in þo.

Hast thou made public another's sin,

  Hast þow any tyme wyth herte prowd
A-noþeres synne I-spoken owt,
And þyn entencyone syche was,
Þat þy synne schulde seme þe las?

or been proud of thine own sins,

Hast þou ben prowde & glad in thoght
Of any mysdede þat þou hast wroȝt?
  Hast þou ben prowde of any gyse
Of any þynge þat þou dedust vse,

or of thy dress, as fools are wont to be,

Of party hosen, of pykede schone,
Of fytered cloþes (as foles done),
Of londes rentes, of gay howsynge,
Of mony seruauntes to þy byddynge,
Or of hors fat and rownde,

or of thy goods, or thy riches,

Or for þy godes were hole & sownde,
Or for þow art gret and ryche
Þat no neȝbore ys þe .I.-lyche,

thy virtue or thy knowledge?

Or for þow art a vertues[2] mon,
And const more þen a-noþer con?
  Ȝef þou haue be on þys maner prowd,

[Fol. 140 back.]

Schryf þe, sone, and telle hyt out.
Hast þou any tyme by veyn glory

Hast thou despised others for being less holy than thyself?

I-þoght þy self so holy,
Þat þow hast had any dedeyn
Of oþer synfulle þat þou hast seyn?

[1] ware. [2] crast.

¶ De accidia.

Hast thou been slow to teach thy godchildren?

HAst þou be slowe, & take non hede
To teche þy godchyldre pater noster & crede?
Haste þow be slowe for to here,
Goddes serues when tyme were?

Hast thou come to church late, and spoken of sin at the gate?

Hast þou come to chyrche late
And spoken of synne by þe gate?
Hast þou be slowe to goddes seruyse,
Or storbet hyt by any wyse?

Hast thou hindered others from going to church, or spoken harlotry within the sanctuary?

Hast þou letted any mon
Þat to chyrche wolde haue gon?
Hast þow spoken harlatry
Wythynne chyrche or seyntwary?
Hath þy herte be wroth or gret
When goddes serues was drawe[1] on tret?
Hast þow hyet hyt to þe ende
Þat þou myȝtes hamward wende?

Hast thou heard sermons without devotion,

Hast þow wyþowte deuocyone
I-herde any predycacyone?
Hast þou gon or seten elles where
When þou myȝtest haue ben þere?

or been loth to fast,

Hast þou be slowe & loth to faste,
When þy herte þere-a-ȝeyn[2] dyde caste?
Hast þou be slowe in any degre
For to do werke of charyte?

or do works of charity?

Hast þou be slowe & feynt in herte
To do penaunce for hyt dyde smerte?

Hast thou neglected pilgrimage?

Hast þou any pylgrimage laft vn-do
When þou were I-ioynet þer-to?
Hast þow by-gunne any dede,
For goddus loue and sowle nede,
Prayerus, penaunce, or fastynge,
Or any oþer holy thynge,

[1] seid. [2] þus to.

[Fol. 141.]

And afterward were so slowe and feynt,
Þat þy deuocyon*e* were all*e* I-queynt?

Hast thou been slow to help thy wife to what she had need of?

Hast þow slowe & feynt I-be
To helpe þy wyf & þy meyne
Of suche as þey hade nede to?
Sey ȝef þow haue so I-do.

If thou art a servant, hast thou done thy duty to thy master?

Ȝef þow be a s*er*uau*n*t,
Hast þow holde þy couenau*n*t?
Hast þow be scharpe and bysy
To serue þy mayster trewely?
Hast þow trewely by vche way
Deseruet þy mete & þy pay?

Hast thou done thy duty to thy neighbour in those matters wherein he trusted thee?

Hath thy neghbore I-trust to þe
To helpe hym in any degre,
And þow, for slowthe & feyntyse,
Hast hym be-gylet in any wyse?

Hast thou given way to despair?

Hath slowþe so I-schent þy þoȝt,
Þat in dyspayre hyt hath þe broȝt,
And neu*er* myȝtest þou non ende make
Of no gode dede þ*at* þ*o*u dydest take?

Hast thou given way to sloth, or neglected to go to church for heat or cold?

Hast þou for slowþe I-be so feynt,
Þat al þy wylle has be weynt,
And soȝt no þyng*e* elles but lust & ese,
And all*e* þat wolde þy body plese?
Hast þ*o*u spared, for hete or colde,
To go to chyrche when þ*o*u were holde?

¶ De invidia.

Hast thou had a grudge against God for anything, or been glad when thy neighbour came to harm?

HAst þow euer be gruchyng*e*
A-gaynes god for any þyng*e*?
Hast þow be in herte glad,
When þy neghbore harme hath had?
Hast þow had in herte gref
Of hys gode and hys relef?

Hast thou envied thy betters,

Hast þow had enuye and erre
To hym þat was þyn ou*er*-herre,

Or any þat was in any degre
I-take forth by-fore the ?

[Fol. 141 back.]

Hast thow enuyet þyn euenyng*e*
For he had euer in any þyng*e*,
Or for he was more abeler þen þow
To alle manere gode and prow ?

or thy equals, that were abler than thou wert,

Hast þow enuyet þyn vnderlyng*e*,
For he was gode and thryuyng*e*,
Or leste he hade I-passed þe
In any vertu or degre ?

or those below thee, because they were thriving ?

Hast þow, for hate or for enuye,
I-holpen or cou*n*selet for to lye
Any mon for to defame,
Or for to destruye hys gode name ?

Hast thou for envy defamed any one,

Hast þow bacbyted þy neghbore
For to make hym fare þe worre ?

or backbitten thy neighbour to make him fare the worse,

Hast þow reret any debate
A-mong*e* þy neȝbor*us* by any hate ?
Hast þow I-sparet for enuye
To teche a mon hys harme to flye,
When þow myȝtest by þy warnyng*e*
Haue hym saued from harmyng*e* ?

or neglected to warn anyone of his danger ?

De ira.

HAst þow, for hate or for yre,
Any þyng*us* set on fuyre ?
Hast þow any tyme be wroth so
Þat þy wyt hath be a-go ?

Hast thou for hate set anything on fire,

or lost thy reason in thine anger ?

Hast þou, by malys of þy doyng*e*,
Wrathþed þy neȝbore in any þyng*e* ?
Hast þow in wrathþe and wyth stryf
I-greuet any crystene lyf ?
Hast þow, wyþ wordes bytter & schrewede,
I-tened any mon, lered or lewede ?
Hast þow, in wraþþe & euel herte,
I-made any mon to smerte ?

Hast thou injured anyone by bitter words ?

Hast þow .I.-corsed or I-blamet,
Or any mon to wrathþe .I.-taimet?

Hast thou slain anyone in thine anger?

Hast þow in wraþþe any mon slayn,
Or holpe þer-to by thy mayn?
Hast þow be wonet to speke ylle

[Fol. 142.]

By any mon, lowde or stylle?

Hast thou been glad to listen unto backbiting?

Hast þow be glad to here bacbyte
Any mon, myche or luyte?

Hast thou cursed anything in thy melancholy, in hope to make it fare worse?

Hast þou any tyme in malencoly
I-corset any þynge bytterly,
In hope to make hyt fare þe worse
By þe malys of thy corse?

Hast thou been impatient at loss of cattle or of friends?

Hast þow be inpacyent
For any gref that god þe sent;
Or elles I-gruched a-gaynes hyt
In herte or worde, oþer in wyt,
As ȝef þy catell fel from the,
Oþer for any infyrmyte,
For los of frendes, or of any þynge,
Or for any syche doynge?

De auaricia.

Hast thou been greedy of gain?

HAst þow wylnet by couetyse
Worldes gode ouer syse,
And spared nother for god ny mon
To gete þat þow fel vp-on?
Hast thow be hard and nythynge
To wythholden any thynge?

Hast thou been hard with borrowers,

Hath any mon vp-on a wedde
Borowet at the oght in nede,
And afterward, when he pay wolde,
Hast þow þenne hys wed wythholde?
For þagh he fayle of hys day,
þow schuldest not hys wed wyþ-say.

or lent anything to gain profit thereby?

Hast þow I-land any thynge
To haue the more wynnynge?

Hast þow I-dronke[1] symonye,
Spyrytual þynge to selle or bye?

Hast thou practised simony?

Hast þow werkemen oght wyth-tan
Of any þynge þat þey schulde han?
Hast þow by-gylet in chafare
Any lyf in lasse or mare?

Hast thou beguiled anyone in bargaining?

Hast þow ȝeue a fals dome
For any mede þat þe come?

Hast thou given any false award to gain by it,

Hast þow falsly be for-swore
For any þyng þow couetest ȝore?

or perjured thyself for the same?

[Fol. 142 back.]

Hast þow I-gete any thynge
Wyth fals countenans and glosynge?
Hast þow I-coueted ouer gate
Worldes worschype or any a-state?

Hast thou coveted over much the world's worship?

Hast þou I-be any executour
To any frende or neghbour,
And drawe out hys gode þe tylle,
And not I-do þe dedes wylle?

Hast thou been an executor and neglected to do the dead person's will?

De gula.

HAst þou I-synget in glotorye?
Telle me, sone, baldelye.

Hast thou been guilty of gluttony,

Hast þow ete wyth syche mayn,
Þat þow hast caste hyt vp a-gayn?

or eaten so greedily that thou hast vomited?

Hast þow wyþ suche vomysment
I-cast vp a-ȝayn þe sacrament?

Hast thou in such vomiting cast up the holy eucharist?

Hast þow be dronke ofte by vse,
And schent þy self by þat vyce?

Hast thou often been drunken,

Hast þou, by malys or by nyste,
I-made any mon dronke to be,
For þou woldest, þe mene whyle,
Any þynge of hym by-gyle,

or made others drunk that thou mightest beguile them out of anything,

Or for þow woldest borde[2] haue,
To se hym dronke and to raue?

or pick sport out of them?

[1] y do. [2] laughter.

Hast thou fasted at proper times?

¶ Hast þou I-fast, as þou schuldest do,
Dayes þat þow were ioynet to,
Or any oþer fastyng*e* day?
Ȝef þow haue do, þou moste say.
Hast þow also for glotory
Ete or dronke to frechedely?[1]

Hast thou eaten and drunken more than need were?

Hast þow ete or dronke more,
Þen þy nede askede fore,
Oþer to erly or to late,
Oþer to swete or delycate?
Ȝef þow haue done þus by vys,
Telle me, sone, for nede hyt ys.

Hast thou cherished thy body with sweet meat and soft clothing?

Hast þow I-chereschet þy body ofte,
In swete met*us* and cloþus softe?

Art thou wont to [Fol. 143.] go to the ale to play the glutton?

Art þow I-wonet to go to þe ale,
To fulle þere thy fowle male,
And drawe þyder oþer wyth þe,
To bere þe feleschype in þat degre?

Hast thou stolen meat or drink?

Hast þou I-stole mete or drynke,
For þou woldest not þ*er*fore swynke?

¶ De luxuria.

Hast thou sinned in lechery?

HAst þow synged in lechery?
Telle me, sone, baldely;
And how ofte þow dydest þat dede,
Telle me þow moste nede;

and was it with wife, maiden, or kindred;

And wheþer hyt were wyf or may,
Sybbe or fremde, þat þow by lay;
And ȝef ho were syb to the,
How syb þow moste telle me;

with ankeress, nun, widow, or any woman vowed to chastity,

And ȝe[f] ho were ankeras or nonne,
Wydowe or wyf, telle ȝef þou conne,
Or any þat haþ a-vowet to chastyte,

or with a common woman?

Or comyn wo*m*mon ȝef ho be,

[1] freshly.

Or wheþ*er* þow dost by strengþe so,
Or by asent of ȝow bo?

Was it with the woman's consent?

Hast þou ete or dronke any letewary
To enforce the to lechery?
Hast þow any þyng*e* wroȝt or do,
Þat stered þy flesch þe more þ*er*to,
Clyppyng*e*, or kyssyng*e*, or towchyng*e* of lyth,
That thy flesch was styred wyth?

Hast thou eaten or drunken anything to enforce to lust? Kissing.

Hast þow be tempted to any wo*m*mon,
And myche & ȝerne I-þoght þer-on,
And woldest fayn in thy þoght,
Þat fowle dede wyþ hyre haue wroȝt?
Þen þow dost sy*n*ne in lechery,
As god hym self seyth v*er*rely;
Wythowte werke or fleschly dede,
Þy chastyte from þe doth flede.

Hast thou much desired to commit this sin,

Hast þow had lust inwardely,
And þoȝt myche in lechery,
And hast be tempted in syche a þoȝt?
Telle me, sone, spare þow noȝt;
Slepyng*e* or wakyng*e*, wheþ*er* hyt were,
Telle me, sone, a-non ryght here.

and thought much on lechery?

[Fol. 143 back.]

Hast þow do sorfet of mete & drynke,
And after we[re] polluted slepynge?
Hast þow do þat synne bale
By any wo*m*mon þat lay in hale?
Hast þow wowet[1] any wyghte,
And tempted hyre ou*er* nyghte?
Hast þou made þe gay þerfore,
Þat heo schulde þe loue þe more?
Hast þou desyred syche to be,
Þat wy*m*men schulde loue þe?
Hast þou hade lykyng*e* for to here
Songes þat of lechery were?

Hast thou tried to seduce any woman,

or taken delight in lustful songs?

[1] wowed.

Hast thou aided anyone in such wicked courses?

Hast þ*ou* cou*n*selet or do socowre
By any wey to a lechowre?
Be-þenke þe, sone, in vche degre
What in þy thoghte be-fel þe;
ȝef þow conne any þyng*e* mynne,[1]
Þat perteneth to þat synne.

Quod si sit femina.

If it be a woman bid her tell thee of what degree the man was that sinned with her; whether he was single or wedded, or a religious,

¶ And ȝef heo be a wo*m*mon,
Byd hyre telle, ȝef heo con,
Of what degre þe mon was
That synned wyþ hyre in þe cas,
Syb or sengul, or any spowse,
Or what degre of relygyowse,

and whether she were ravished or consented thereto,

Or wheþ*er* hyt were a-gayn hyre wylle,
Or wheþ*er* heo a-sented fully þer-tylle,

and whether she did it for pay, for then the sin double were.

Or wheþ*er* hyt were for couetyse
Of gold or selu*er*, or oght of hyse,
Þenne þe synne dowbul were,
And neded penawnce myche more.
Why & where, how & whenne,
And how ofte, aske hyre þenne;
Of alle poyntes þow moste wyte,
As by-fore .I. haue wryte.

¶ De modo inquirendi de peccatis venialibus.

Of venial sins.

NOw of synnes venyal,
A luyte[2] aske þe I schal:

Hast thou spent thy wits in God's [Fol. 144.] service?

Hast þow spende þy wytt*us* fyue
To godd*us* worschype? telle me blyue.
Þese ben þey, as .I. þe telle,
Towche & tast, & eke þy smelle,
Þy heryng*e* also and þy syȝt;
Here þey be fyue on ryȝt.

[1] nyme. [2] litul.

¶ De visu.

Hast thou seen anything that enticed thee to sin,

¶ Hast þow .I.-seyn any thynge
þat tysed þe to synnynge?
Be-þenke þe, sone, welle .I. pray
For mony þyngus þat falle may.

¶ De auditu.

or had a liking to listen to evil,

¶ Hast þow .I.-had gret lykynge
For to here euele thynge,
Or nyce wordes of rybawdy,
Or suche maner harlotry?

¶ De olfactu.

or smelt anything, such as meat, drink, or spicery, that has led thee to sin?

¶ Hast þow .I.-smelled any þynge
þat hath tend thy lykynge,
Of mete or drynke or spysory,
þat þow hast after .I.-synned by?

¶ De gustu.

Hast thou sinned in thy eating?

¶ Also ȝef þou synned hast,
In mete or drynke by lusty tast,
þat also þow moste telle me,
ȝef .I. schale a-soyle the.

¶ De tactu.

Hast thou sinned in touching anything that thou shouldest not?

¶ Hast þou .I.-towched folyly,
þat þy membrus were styred by,
Wommones flesch or þyn owne?
ȝef þow hast, þou moste schowne.
Here ben þe wyttus fyue,
How þey ben spende, telle me blyue,
And whad þou hast in herte more,
Telle me, sone, a-non by-fore:
I praye þe, sone, be not a-ferde,
But telle hyt owte now a-pert.
Telle me, sone, I the pray,

I wole þe helpe ȝef þat I may.

Hast thou done all thy penances?

¶ Is þy penaunce alle I-do,
þat þy schryffader ioynet þe to?

Dost thou forgive all that have trespassed against thee?

For-gyuest þow wyth herte fre,
Alle þo þat haue trespaset to þe?

Hast thou kept all vows that thou hast made?

Any vow hast þow .I.-mad?
Hast þou þat holden ferme and sad?

[Fol. 144 back.]

Hast thou eaten on Sundays without holy bread?

Hast þow eten any sonday
With-owte halybred? say ȝe, or nay.

Hast thou disturbed priest or clerk at his work?

Hast þou I-storbet prest or clerk
þat were bysy in goddes werk?
Hast þou I-had or wyst where,
þat was I-asked in chyrche þere?

Hast thou wished thyself accursed?

Hast þow wyþowte knowlachynge
I-wyst þe a-corsed for any þynge?

Art thou wont to make plays at any likewake?

Art þow I-wont at lychwake
Any pleyes for to make?

Hast thou done works of mercy?

þe werkes of mercy summe & alle,
Hast þou I-wroȝt, as þe by-felle?

Hast thou helped to bury the dead?

¶ Hast þow holpe by þy myȝt
To burye þe dede, as byd owre dryȝt?

Hast thou succoured the poor?

Pore & naked and hongry,
Hast þow I-sokeret mekely?

Hast thou done kindly deeds to the sick prisoners and wayfarers?

Hast þou in herte rowþe I-had,
Of hem þat were nede be-stad,
To seke & sore and prisonerus
I-herberet alle weyferus?

Hast thou quarrelled with thy wife?

Hast þou I-lyued also in chost & stryf
Wyþ þy meyne and wyþ þy wyf?

Have thou and she overlain any of your infants?

Hast þow also by hyre I-layn,
And so by-twene ȝow þe chylde I-slayn?

Hast thou kept thy children in subjection?

Also þy chyldre þat were schrewes,
Hast þow I-taght hem gode þewes?

Hast thou overheld corn?

Hast þow ouer-holde corne or ote,[1]
Or oþer þynge þat come neuer to note?

[1] wote.

For to lene, hast þow be loth,
And for to quite, hast þou be wroth?
¶ Hast þow be in corset cumpany
Of corset men? telle me why,
To socour hem wyþ bodyly fode,
Or to preche hem for here gode?
Who so sokereth hem in here malys,
He ys as corsed as þey I-wys.
Telle also for the bet,
Matrymony ȝef þow haue let.
Hast þow I-come by chyrche ȝorde,
And for þe dede I-prayed no worde?
Hast þow ay cast vp lyde ȝate
Þere bestus haue go in ate?
Hast þow I-struyed corn or gras,
Or oþer þynge þat sowen was?
Hast þou I-come in any sty,
And cropped ȝerus of corne[1] þe by?
Art þou I-wont ouer corn to ryde,
When þou myȝtest haue go by syde?
Ȝef þow haue more in herte,
Telle me, sone, now alle smerte;
For alle þat þow helest now fro me
Þe fende fulle redyly wole telle þe.
But when he con no more sayn,
Þen ȝeue hym penaunce withowte layn.

Hast thou frequented the company of cursed men, to succour them, or to preach to them for their good?

Hast thou hindered matrimony?
[Fol. 145.]

Hast thou passed by a churchyard and neglected to pray for the dead?

Hast thou ever left open a gate so that beasts have gone in?

Hast thou destroyed corn, grain, or other things that were sown?

Art thou wont to ride over corn?

¶ De modo iniungendi penitenciam.

Now, confessour, I warne þe,
Here connynge þow moste be;
Wayte þat þow be slegh & fel
To vnderstonde hys schryft wel;
Wherfore þese þynges þow moste wyte
That in þys vers nexte be wryte.

Of the manner of enjoining penance.

[1] MS. corner.

¶ Quis, quid, vbi, per quos, quociens, quomodo, quando.

You must bear in mind who the penitent is;

¶ Fyrst þow moste þys mynne,[1]
What he ys þat doth þe synne,

whether young or old, bond or free, poor or rich,

Wheþer hyt be heo or he,
ȝonge or olde, bonde or fre,
Pore or ryche, or in offys,
Or mon of dygnyte ȝef he ys,

single or married, clerk or secular person,

Sengul or weddet, or cloystrere,
Clerke, or lewed, or seculere,
Byschope or prest, or mon of state,
þow moste wyte þese al gate.
 þe herre þat a mon ys in degre,
þe sarrer forsoþe falleþ he;

and whether he be in his wits or no.

And ȝef he were in hys wyt,
Also þow moste wyte hyt.
What synne hyt ys, and how I-wroȝt,

[Fol. 145 back.] You must be heedful to know all his sin,

To wyte redyly, spare þow noght;
Wheþer hyt be gret or smal,
Open or hud, wyte þow al.
Lechery, robbery, or monslaȝt,
Byd hym telle euen straȝt.

for some will not tell all their sin.

For summe telleþ not here synne al,
In confessyone general.
þus a mon may other whyle
þe and hym boþe by-gyle.

It is not sufficient for the penitent to say he has slain a man; he must say who he was, wherefore, and why.

Hyt ys to luyte for any mon
To say he hath slayn a mon.
But ȝef he telle hyt openly,
What mon he was, wharfore, & why,
Wheþer hyt be fader or broþer,
Prest or clerke, or any other.

A man who has sinned in lechery must not mention

 Also men sayn comynly
I haue synned in lechery,

[1] nyme.

ȝet most þow wyte by whom hyt ys,
Or elles ȝe mowe do boþe a-mys.
But nome he schal non telle þe;
But ȝef þe synne syche be,
Þat he ne may hys schryfte telle,
But he take hyre in hys spelle,
Þen he may þe name mynge.
Ellus hym aȝte for no þynge;

the name of the other person unless it be needful.

But wheþ*er* he be wyf or may,
Syb or fremde, make hym say,
Nonne or ankeras, or what degre,
Algate make hym telle the;
For ȝef þe synne be gret or grym,
Þe more penau*n*ce nedeth hym.

But he must tell in what state and condition of life she was,

Were hyt was, wyte þ*o*u also
In holy place or no.
A mon synneþ sarre in seyntwary
Þenne in any oþer place by,
By whom also þow moste mynne,
And whom he gart to do þat synne,
And whad þey were þ*at* were here fer*us*,
Prestes or clerk*us*, monkes or frerus,
Þe mo to synne that he droghe,
Þe more for-sothe hym-self he sloghe.

and whether or not the sin was done in a holy place,

[Fol. 146.]

How ofte also he dyde that dede,
Wyte at hym þow moste nede,
For eu*er* so ofter newed hyt ys,
Þe g*ra*tter þe synne waxeth I-wys;
So ofter a wou*n*de ys I-cot,
Þe worse to hele hyt nede be mot;
Þe ofter a mon doth monslaghte,
Þe more he ys the fende by-taghte;
Þe ofter he doth lechery,
Þe ofter he synneth dedly;
Dedly he synneth, wyþowte drede,
As ofte as he þat synne doþ brede,

and how often the sin was done, for the oftener it is done the more the sin is.

And why he dyde þat ylke synne,
Also nede he mote mynne:

He must also say whether he sinned for love or fear.

Wheþ*er* hyt were for loue or drede,
Or couetyse of worldes mede,
Or for enuye, or for debate,
Or for wrathþe of olde hate,
And he dyde, he mote say,
And not hele hyt by no way:
Wheþ*er* he dyde þat in hastynes,
Or wel a-vyset ȝef he wes;
For he þ*at* casteth hym to do a dede,
More penaun*c*e he mote haue nede
Þen he þ*at* doth hyt sodenlyche,
And afterward*e* hym reweth myche;

He must say on what day he sinned, for a sin done on a holy day or fasting day is worse than one committed at another time.

And whe*n*ne hyt was, and what day,
Byd hym to the that he say;
For on a halyday ȝef he synne,
Nedely to þe he mote hyt mynne,
Or any oþer fastyng*e* day,
Lentu*n* or vygyle, as telle he may;

[Fol. 146 back.]

For gratt*er* synne for soþe hyt ys
On suche dayes to do a-mys,
Myche more wythoute nay,
Þen on a-noþ*er* werkeday;
And ȝet more by-fore none
Þen aft*er*ward*e* and hyt were done;
Þ*er*fore þou moste wel hyt mynne,
Boþe tyde & tyme, he þ*at* doth synne.

All these things must be known, or else the confessor cannot give a good dome.

Alle þese poynt*us* þow moste wyte,
Þ*at* here be-fore ben .I.-wryte;
Or elles gode dome þou myȝt not ȝeue
Of men þat beth to the .I.-schryue,
So þow myȝt knowe su*m* and al,
Wheþ*er* þe synne be gret or smal,

If the sin be great, so must the penance be.

And ȝef þe synne be fowle & grym,
The gr*a*tter penaun*c*e ȝeue þou hym;

And ȝef þe synne be but luyte,
To þe lasse penaunce þou hym putte;
But fyrst take hede, by gode a-vys,
Of what contrycyone þat he ys,
Ȝef he be sory for hys synne,
And fulle contryte as þou myȝt kenne;
Wepeþ faste, and ys sory,
And asketh ȝerne of mercy,
A-bregge hys penaunce þen by myche,
For god hym self for-ȝeueth syche.
Ȝef he be styf & of herte heȝ,
Grope hym softe, & go hym neȝ,
And when þou herest where he wole byde,
Ȝeue hym penaunce þenne also þat tyde,
But non oþer þen he wole take
Wors þenne lest þow hym make.
Take gode hede on hys de-gre,
Of what skynnes[1] lyuyuge þat he be;
For on may soffre þat a-noþer ne may,
Þerfore set hym in syche way,
Þat hys penaunce he may do ryȝt,
Be hyt heuy, be hyt lyȝt;
Ȝef þow ley on hym more
Þenne he wole asente fore,
Alle he wole caste hym fro,
And schende hym-self, .I. telle þe so,
Wharfore be wys and war,
For mony men fulle dyuers ar.
Now take hede what .I. þe mynne,
Ȝef a wyf haue done a synne,
Syche penaunce þou gyue hyre þenne
Þat hyre husbonde may not kenne,
Leste for þe penaunce sake
Wo & w[r]aþþe by-twene hem wake.

If the sin be light, let the penance be light also.

If the man is sorry for his sin, let the penance be abridged;

but if he be stiff of heart the penance must be heavy,

but still such as he will perform;

[Fol. 147.]

for if a man has more laid on him than he will do, he will cast it all aside and be worse than if he had not gone to confession.

A woman's penance must be such as her husband may not know.

[1] kynnes.

Wharfore þe nedeth to be wys,
For, forsothe, gret nede hyt ys,
Lest þow do oȝt on madhede,
And sende so al to þe quede;
Bett*ur* hyt ys wyth penau*n*ce lutte,
In-to purgatory a mon to putte,
Þen wyþ penau*n*ce ouer myche,
Sende hym to helle putte.[1]
Wharfore lerne þys lessou*n* wel,
And take gode hede to my spel,
Cou*n*t*ur* wyþ cou*n*t*ur* ys .I.-huled ofte,
When þey be leyde to-ged*ur* softe.

Better with a light penance to send a man to purgatory, than with penance overmuch to send him to hell.

¶ **Contra superbiam.**

Agayn*us* pruyde, wythowte les,
Þe forme remedy ys mekenes:
Ofte to knele, and erþe to kys,
And knowlache wel þat erþe he ys,
And dede menn*us* bon*us* ofte to se,
And þenke þat he schal syche be.
Þe peynes of helle haue ȝerne in thoȝt,
And domes day for-ȝete thow noght;
Cryst*us* passyon*e* haue in mynde;
Þat sleth pruyde, as wryten .I. fynde,
And who so þenketh þus in stedefast thoȝt,[2]
Pruyde he schale sette at noȝt.

Pride. The remedy for it is meekness.

It is good for thee to kiss the earth and look on dead men's bones, and think on the pains of hell and Christ's passion.

[Fol. 147 back.]

¶ **Contra Iram.**[3]

Agaynes wraþþe hys helpe schal be,
Ȝef he haue grace in herte to se
How au*n*gel*us*, when he ys wroth,
From hym faste flen and goth,
And fendes faste to hym renneth,
And wyþ fuyre of helle hys herte breneth,

Wrath. Against this sin the remedy is for a man to see how angels flee from him when he is angry, and fiends fast to him run and burn his heart with hell-fire;

[1] pitche. [2] The above four lines are not in Douce 103. [3] MS. *Iiram*.

And maketh hym so hote & hegh,
Þat no mon may byde hym negh,
And makeþ hym syche as þey arn,
Of goddes chylde, þe deueles barn,

and make him such as they are—of God's child the devil's bairn.

Wharfore he mote wyth sofferyng*e*,
Quenche in hym syche brennyng*e*,
A-gayn*us* wrathþe soferau*n*ce
Mote be myche hys penau*n*ce.

¶ Contra Inuidiam.

Envy.

AGayn enuye, loue ys gryth,
But ȝet he mote do more wyth,
Serues to hym wyth herte fre
To whom he hath enuyes .I.-be.
Louyng*e* s*er*ues and godely speche,
Agayn enuye ys helpe and leche.

¶ Contra auariciam.

Covetousness.

DO also in thys wyse,
I bydde, a-ȝeynes couetyse:
Quyte a-gayn (a-byde not to longe),
Þat þow hast take wyth wronge,
And to þe nedy ȝeue þow large,
In godd*us* name .I. þe charge.

¶ Contra gulam.

Gluttony.

OF þy fowle gloterye
Abstene þe, .I. bydde þe hye;
And for þy lust & þy sorfet
Þow moste do almes full*e* gret;
Fede þe pore of þat þow sparest,
And lete hem fele how þow farest.

¶ Contra accidiam.

¶ Slowthe þow moste to gode t*ur*ne,
And þy pat*er* noster say ȝerne,
In morowe & mydday & euentyde,
Wheþ*er* þow go oþer þow ryde.

[Fol. 148.] Sloth. The remedy is to say the pater noster at morn, midday, and eventide;

To chyrche come, ȝef þow may,
And here þy masse vche day;
And ȝef þow may not come to chyrche,
Where euer þat þow do worche,
When þow herest to masse knylle,
Prey to god wyþ herte stylle,
To ȝeue þe part of þat s*er*uyse,
Þat in chyrche I-done ys.

to hear mass each day, and if work hinders from going to church, to join in heart in the service when the mass knell is heard.

¶ Contra luxuriam.

Lechery.

Thagh þow þenke þy lechery swete,
Lef þow hyt, .I. the hete,
And lerne to lyue in chastyte,—
In goddes name .I. charge þe;—
And for þy flesch þ*er*-in has game,
Wi*th* bred & wat*er* þou schalt hyt tame;
And ȝef he say a-gayn to þe,
He may not lyue in chastyte,
Charge hym þenne to take a wyf,
In goddes lawe to lede hys lyf;
And þaȝ he say he wole not do so,
Ȝet penau*n*ce make hym to do;
Hyt schale do gode here or henne,
Laske hys peynes, or cese hys synne.

Tame the flesh by bread and water.

He who cannot live in chastity to take a wife.

¶ Quanta sit penitencia pro mortalibus.

The legal penance for mortal sin.

On dedly synne, as lawes techeth,
To seuen ȝerus ende recheth,
Faste bred & wat*er* vche fryday,
And for-go flesch on wednesday,
The same dayes þorȝ þe ȝere,
That schal laste fully seuen ȝere;
But now be fewe þat wole do so,
Þ*er*fore a lyȝter way þou moste go;
A mo*n*nes cont*ri*cyon*e* be-holde þou ȝerne,
Þer-by þy domes thow moste lerne;

There are now few who will perform it.

ȝef hyt be gret, ȝeue luyte penau*n*ce.
ȝef hyt be luyte, þow moste hyt vau*n*ce,[1]
[Fol. 148 back.]
Be hyt more, be hyt lasse,
Aft*er* þe cont*r*icyon*e* þe dome moste passe.
Be not to harde, .I. þe rede,
But ay do m*er*cy in goddes drede,
He ys ful of me[r]cy ay,
Be þ*o*u also, I the pray;
For lasse synnes venyal,
Light penance to be given for venial sin.
Lasse penau*n*ce ȝeue þow schal,
So þat þe synne hys herte greue,
And be in purpose hyt to leue.
I hope here be .I.-noȝ .I.-wryte,
To teche a pr*e*st how he schale wyte,
To ȝeue a dome of mo*n*nes synne,
ȝef any wyt be hym wyþynne.

¶ Isti mittendi sunt ad episcopum.

Cases reserved for the bishop:
Bvt, confesso*ur*, be wys and ȝop,
And sende forth þese to þe byschop:
All that smite priests or clerks, house-burners, murderers, mothers that overlie their children;
Alle þat smyteþ pr*e*st or clerk,
And hem þ*a*t worcheþ wycked werk,
Hows-brenner & sleer of mon,
And fader or mod*ur* in vyolens[2] þ*a*t leyþ hond vp-on,
Þe mod*ur* þat þe chylde ou*er* lyth,
Þe fader also sende þow wyth,
a man cursed with book and bell; heretics, vow-breakers, coin-clippers, usurers, false witnesses, and folk that have been unlawfully wedded;
A mon þat ys a-corset wyþ book & belle,
And eretykes, as .I. the telle;
Hym þat brekeþ solempne vow,
Or chawnge hyt wole, sende hym forþ now;
Clypper of þe kynges mynt,
And hym þat lyueth by swerdes dynt
Alle fals sysour*us* and okerer*us*,
And hem þat fals wytnes ber*us*;

[1] haunce.
[2] "in vyolens" must be a later insertion, as it makes the line too long.

Alle þat be wedded vnlawfully,
Or susterus or cosynus lyggeþ by;
And alle þo, schortely to say,
Þat þe grete sentens a-corseþ ay;
And ȝef þe byschope a-corse mo,
Sende hem forth-wyth also.

those who have lain with sisters or cousins; and all that are cursed by the great excommunication.

[Fol. 149.]

¶ De modo absoluendi penitentem.

Absolution: how it is given.

NOw take hede how þow schalt done
Of thyn absolucyone;
When schryfte ys herde, þen ȝeue penaunce,
And bydde hym say wyth fulle creawnce:

¶ Et dicat confitens.

A form of confession.

"GOd, .I. crye þe mercy,
And þy moder seynt mary,
And alle þe seyntus of heuen bryȝt,
I crye mercy wyth alle my myȝt,
Of alle þe synnus I haue wroȝt,
In werke and worde, & sory þoȝt,
Wyth euery lyme of my body,
Wyth sore herte I aske god mercy,
And þe, fader, in goddes place,
A-soyle me þow of my trespace,
Ȝeue me penaunce also to,
For goddes loue þat þow so do."

¶ Tunc dicat sacerdos.

The form of absolution.

EGo, auctoritate dei patris omnipotentis & beatorum[1] apostolorum petri & pauli, & officij michi commissi in hac parte, absoluo te ab hijs peccatis michi per te confessis, & ab alijs de quibus non recordaris. In nomine patris & filij & spiritus sancti. Amen. Ista humilitas & passio domini nostri ihesu christi

[1] *beatorum* not in Douce 103.

& m*er*ita s*anc*te mat*r*is eccl*es*ie, & o*mn*es indulgencie tibi concesse, & om*n*ia bona que fecisti & facies vsq*ue* in fine*m* vite tue, sint tibi in remissionem istor*um* & omniu*m* al*ior*um pecc*at*or*um* tuor*um*. Amen.

¶ De sacramento extreme vnccionis.

Extreme unction

Hyt ys not gode to be helut,
How a wyȝt schal be an-elet.
When þ*at* he ys so ou*er*-dryue
þat he may no leng*ur* lyue,
þenne he schale an-elet be,
And non er, .I. warne the;
But þaȝ he be an-elet ones,
ȝet he may eftsones;
But he þat ys in hys wyt,
And be so temptut, despyseþ hyt,
Haue he in herte non oþ*er* mynne,
He schale be dampned for þ*at* synne;
But he þ*at* schale be an-oynt,
Aske hym þus eu*er*y poynt:

to be given when a man is near death.

He who despises this sacrament will be damned.

[Fol. 149 back.]

Infirmus dicta ȝe.

Questions to be asked of the sick person.

¶ "Art þow fayn, my broþer, say,
þat þow dyest in crysten fay?
Myȝt þou also in þy herte se
þat þy lyf ys worse þen hyt scholde be?" ȝe.
"For-þynkeþ þe, telle me þys,
þat þou hast lad þy lyf a-mys?" ȝe.
"Hast þow wyl þe to a-mende,
ȝer god wole þe lyf sende?" ȝe.
"Be-leuest þow w*ith* ful gode deuocyon*e*
On ih*es*u crystes passyone?" ȝe.
"And how hys passyon*e* saue þe schal,
And by non oþer way at al?" ȝe.
Holde vp now boþe þy hondes
And þonke c*r*iste of alle hys sondes,

Dost thou die in the Christian faith?

Has thy life been worse than it should be?

Hast thou lived amiss?

Hast thou a will to amend if thy life be spared?

Believest thou on the Lord's passion?

And how it alone can save thee?

Hold up both hands and thank Christ, and pray

him for his mother's sake that he will take thy soul.

And praye hym, for hys moder sake,
Þat he wole þy sowle take
In-to hys honde and hys kepynge,
And saue hyt from þe fowle þynge.
  Ȝef he con þys oresone say,
Byd hym say hyt wyþowte delay:—

¶ **Oracio dicenda ab infirmo ante vnccionem.**

Prayer to be said by the sick man.

DEus meus, deus meus, misericordia mea & refugium meum, te desidero, ad te confugio, ad te festino venire. ne despicias me sub tremendo discrimine positum; adesto michi propicius in hijs magnis meis necessitatibus: non possum me redimere meis operacionibus. Sed tu, deus meus, redime me & miserere mei. diffido de meis meritis, sed magis confido de miseracionibus tuis & plus confido de miseracionibus tuis quam diffido de malis meis actibus. tu spes mea, deus meus, tibi soli peccaui; mea culpa, mea maxima culpa! nunc ad te venio quia nulli dees; cupio dissolui & esse tecum. In manus tuas domine commendo spiritum meum, redemisti me domine, deus veritatis. Amen. Et patra michi, deus meus, vt in pace dormiam & requiescam. Qui in trinitate perfecta viuis & regnas deus, per omnia[1] secula seculorum. Amen.

¶ **Tunc vngatur infirmus.**

Further instructions to men of mean lore.

ȜEt I wole wryte more,
  To hym þat ys mene of lore,

Of negligence that may befal in the mass.

Of neclygens, more & lasse,
Þat may be-falle in þe masse.

A priest who says mass must be out of deadly sin. [Fol. 150.]

  Fyrst se, prest, as I þe mynne,
Þat þow be out of dedly synne;
Þyn auter þenne þou do dyȝt,
Þat hyt be after thy myȝt.

[1] infinita.

Se þe cloþes þat þey be clene,
And also halowet alle by-dene;

The altar cloths must be clean, and all of them hallowed.

Wyth þre towayles, and no lasse,
Hule þyn auter at thy masse.

Three towels to be on the altar at mass.

Al oþer thynge þow knowest wel,
What þe nedeth euer-.y. del:—
Loke þat þy candel of wax hyt be,

The candle to be of wax,

And set hyre, so þat þow hyre se,
On þe lyfte half of þyn autere,
And loke algate ho brenne clere,

and to burn clearly.

Wayte þat ho brenne in alle wyse,
Tyl þow haue do þat seruyse.
Þy bred schal be of whete flour,

The bread to be of wheaten flour.

I-made of dogh that ys not sour;
Þat hyt be rounde and hol, wayte wel,
And loke þy wyn be not eysel;

The wine not sour.

Poure water to thy wyn,

Water to be put to the wine.

As þow const, wel and fyn;
Sey þe wordes of þat seruyse
Deuowtely wyth gode a-vyse;
Cotte þow not þe wordes tayle,

The tails of the words not to be cut.

But sey hem oute wyþowte fayle;
Sey hem so wyþ mowþe & thoght,
Þat oþer þynge þow þenke noght,
But al þyn herte & þyn entent
Be fully on that sacrament.
Ȝef hyt be-falle, as god hyt scylde,

If it happen, through accident, that bread or wine be not on the altar when mass is being said, lay bread on the corporax, and begin again at "qui pridie."

Þat þow of wyt be so wylde,
Þat bred or wyn be a-way,
Consecracyone when þou scholdest say;
Ȝef þe be-falle þat ylke cas,
Ley bred on þy corporas,
And þaȝ þow forth .I.-passet be,
Be-gynne a-gayn " qui pridie."
Ȝef wyn and water be bothe a-way,

[Fol. 150 back.]

Powre in boþe wythowte lay,

If wine and water are absent,

supply them, and begin at "simili modo."

And t*ur*ne a-gayn, as I þe kenne,
And "simili modo" say þow þe*n*ne.

If you have water and no wine, supply it, and begin again at the same place.

ȝef þou haue wat*er* and no wyn,
A-non-ryȝt do hyt yn,
And by-gy*n*ne, as .I. ȝer taȝte,
At "simili modo" euen straȝte;
And ȝef þow be neȝ þe ende,
ȝef syche mynde god þe sende,
Þat þow haue wyn & no water,
Þen powre hyt in neu*er* þe later,
And by-gynne "oremus,
Preceptis salutarib*us*."

If you have forgotten stole or fannon go forth for them.

ȝef þe wonte stole or fanou*n*,
When þow art in þe canou*n*,
Passe forth wythowten turne,
But þat þow moste rewe ȝerne;

If a drop of blood fall on the corporax, suck it up, and be as sorry as you can for it, and put the corporax away among the relics.

ȝef a drope of blod by any cas
Falle vp-on þe corporas,
Sowke hyt vp a-non-ryȝt,
And be as sory as þou myȝt;
Þe corporas, after þow folde,
A-mong*e* þe relek*us* to be holde;
On oþer þyng*e* ȝef hyt falle,
On vestement oþ*er* on palle,
A-wey þow moste þe pece cotte,
And[1] & a-mong*e* þe relek*us* putte;

If it fall on anything else, lick it up and shave the place, and burn the shavings and put the ashes among the relics.

ȝef hyt falle on su*m* oþ*er* what,
Tabul or ston, vrþe or mat,
Lyk hyt vp clene þat ys sched,
And schaf hyt after, þat ys be-bled,
And do þe schauyng*e* for to brenne,
Among*e* þe relek*us* put hyt þenne.

If a gnat, fly, or spider fall into the cup, swallow it.

ȝef any flye, gnat, or coppe,
Dou*n* in-to þe chalys droppe,

[1] MS. "And hyt brenne." The "hyt brenne" must be a later insertion, from l. 1823, as it makes the line too long.

ȝef þow darst for castyng*e* þere,
Vse hyt hol all*e* .I.-fere,
And ȝef þy herte do wyþstonde,
Take vp the fulþe wyþ þyn honde,
And ou*er* the chalys wosche hyt wel
Twyes or thryes, as .I. þe telle,
And vse forth þe blod þenne,
And do þe fulþe for to brenne.
  Do more ȝet also thow most,
Vche day chawu*n*ge þyn ost,
Redy þat þow haue mowe,
To vche seke ay .I.-nowe.

[Fol. 151.]

If you are afraid of vomiting, take it out with your hand and wash it over the chalice and then burn it.

Change the host each day.

¶ Ad-huc alia necessaria capellano scire.

ȝEt lerne þys for thy prow,
  Þat .I. wryte aft*er* now.
When þow schalt to seke gon,
Hye þe faste & go a-non;
For ȝef þow tarye, þow dost a-mys,
Þow schalt quyte that sowle .I.-wys.
When þow schalt to seke gon,
A clene surples caste þe on;
Take þy stole wyth þe, ryȝt,
And pul thy hod ou*er* þy syȝt;
Bere þyn ost a-nont þy breste,
In a box that ys honeste.
  Make þy clerk be-fore þe ȝynge,
To bere lyȝt, and belle rynge;
On þy power þen haue þow mynne,
Þat þow myȝt a-soyle of alle synne;
In perel of deth þow hast powere,
Of alle synne to a-soyle clere;
But ȝef þe seke t*ur*ne to lyue,
Of þat same synne he mote hym schryue,
And hys penau*n*ce take newe,
For alle þyng*e* þat he er schewe.

Go fast to the sick.

When thou goest put on a clean surplice, take thy stole with thee, and pull thy hood over thy eyes.

Bear the host on thy breast.

Cause the clerk to bear a light and ring a bell before thee.

In peril of death thou hast the power to assoil from all sin.

Spare not to ask the sick of his sins.

[Fol. 151 back.]

And spare þow not for no let
To aske hym of hys det;
And whether hyt be myche or luyte,
Charge hym þat he hyt quyte;
And ȝef hys godes to luyte be
For to quyte þat oweth he,

Charge him with lowly heart to ask mercy.

Charge hym þenne, wyth herte lowe,
To aske mercy of þat he owe.
And ȝet þow moste lerne þys eke,
Of a mon þat ys ful seke,
Þat sendeþ to þe to hym to ryde,

If a sick man cannot speak, but by signs shews that he wishes for the housel and holy oil, they are to be given to him.

And waxe dowmbe in þat tyde,
Ȝef he by synes þat hosul soghte,
Thaȝ þow knowe, þow schryue hym noȝte,
Nerþeles þow schalt hym soyle,
And ȝeue hym hosul & holy oyle.
When þou hast þe seke .I.-schryue,
And þow se þat he may not lyue,

The sick person to have no other penance given but his sickness.

Oþer penaunce þow schalt not gyn
But þe sekenes þat he ys In,
Ioyne þat sekenes & þat sore
By-fore god to be hys ore;
And ȝef he aske hys sauyour,
Gyf hym hyt wyþ gret honour;

If he is so sick that he would vomit up the holy eucharist, it is not to be given to him, but he is to be told that the desire for it is sufficient.

But ȝef he be so seke wyth-ynne
Þat of castynge he may not blynne,
He schalt not þenne hys hosul take,
For vomyschment & castynge sake,
But preche hym feyre wyth opun spelle
Þat god a-loweth hys herte & hys wylle;
And for he wolde & he myȝte,
God hym takeþ in hys ryȝte.
Ȝef when þou art to chyrche .I.-went,
Do vp so that sacrament

The host to be made secure in church, so that

[Fol. 152.]

Þat hyt be syker in vche way,
Þat no best hyt towche may.

ȝef hyt [were] eten wyth mows or rat,
Þere þow moste a-bygge þat;
Fowrty dayes for þat myschawnce
Þow schalt be in penaunce.

no mouse or rat may eat it.

ȝef any crome of hyt be lost,
ȝerne seche hyt þow most;
ȝef þow hyt fynde no wey myȝte,
Þrytty dayes þow rewe hyt ryȝte;

If any crumb of it be lost it must be sought for.

And ȝef þow be so vnwys
Þat þow synge by malys,
Wythowte water and lyȝt also,
And wost welle þe wonteth bo,
Þow schalt þenne, for þy songe,
Boþe wepe and weyle er a-monge,
Tyl þe byschope of hys ore
To þy songe the restore.

If through malice thou singest mass without water and a light, thou must do penance till the bishop restore thee.

¶ Oracio opificis opusculi huius.

NOw, dere prest, .I. pray þe,
For goddes loue þow pray for me;
More .I. pray þat þow me mynge,
In þy masse when thow dost synge;

The priest to pray for the author, and to remember him when he sings mass.

And ȝet .I. pray þe, leue broþer,
Rede þys ofte, and so lete oþer,
Huyde hyt not in hodymoke,
Lete other mo rede þys boke;
The mo þer-In doth rede & lerne,
Þe mo to mede hyt schale terne;
Hyt ys I-made hem to schowne
Þat haue no bokes of here owne,
And oþer þat beth of mene lore,
Þat wolde fayn conne more;

This book is made to instruct those who have no books of their own, and others of mean lore.

And þow þat here-In lernest most,
Thonke ȝerne þe holy gost,
That ȝeueþ wyt to vche mon
To do þe gode that he con,

[Fol. 152 back.]

And by hys tr*a*uayle and hys dede
ȝeueþ hym heuen to hys mede; 1932
The mede and þe ioye of heuen lyȝt,
God vs gr*a*unte For hys myght. Amen.

Explicit tractatus qui d*icitu*r pars oculi, de latino in anglicum tr*a*nslatus per f*rat*rem Ioh*ann*em myrcus, canonicu*m* regularem Monasterij de Lylleshul, cui*us* a*nim*e p*ro*picietu*r* deus! Ame*n*.

THE POINTS AND ARTICLES OF CURSING.

(Cotton MS. Claudius A ii. Leaf 123 back, after Mirc's Festial.)

¶ De magna sentencia, pronuncianda hoc modo.

(*The few verses at the beginning are written like prose.*)

ÞE grete sente*n*s I wryte þe here,
þ*at* foure tymes in þe ȝere
þou schalte [1] pronownce with-owtyn lette,
Whan þe parich is to-gydur mette:
þou schalte p*ro*nownce þis [2] hydowse þinge
Wit cros and candul, and belle knyllynge,
þe furste sononday affter myȝhell feste;
Mydlenton sonday schal be neste;
þe trenite feste is þe þridde, os I þe say;
þe ferthe is þe sononday aftur candulmes day:
Sepelle [3] hit reddely, for noȝte þou wonde,
þ*at* alle men þe vndurstonde.

[1] MS. þou schalte þou schalte. [2] this D, *om.* C. [3] Spelle D.

[*The Address.*]

¶ Gode men, þeis poyntus and arti[c]les þ*at* I wille schewe ȝow of cursyng*e*, bene stabullud & ordeynud & confermed of popus & byschoppus & prelatus of holy chirche, & commawnded & chard[g]ud þ*at* alle þoo þ*at* haue cure of mann*us* sowle off here paryschonus, þ*at* þei, fowre tymes in þe ȝere, þeis poyntus & articles off cursynge schewe here paryschon*us*, [1] þ*at* þei, thorogh knowinge, no defawte off techinge, falle in-to no cursynge. ¶ For, rythe os a swerde de-partuth þe heued frome þe body. ¶ Ryȝte so, gostelyche to speke, thoroghe prestus tonge, þ*at* is goddus swerde, to vndurstonde, departeth mann*us* sowle —þ*at* ih*es*u cryste (goddus sonne) bowte wit his worthy blode a-pone þe rode-treo—fro hym & fro oure lady, & ffro alle þe cu*m*pany of heuen; And he takuth hit to þe fende off helle, & to hys mynestrees, to þe peyne of helle, al so longe os god is in heuen. ¶ And there-fore I ȝow bydde & charge, for þe loff of cryste, & savaysione off ȝoure sowles, þ*at* ȝe vndurstand welle alle þeis poyntus. ¶ And ȝif any off ȝow feluth hym gylty in any of alle þeis, þ*at* he hym amende þorogh schryfte and penaunce, and þ*at* be tyme.

[*The Curse.*]

¶ Be þe auctorite of our lorde ih*es*u cryste, & off oure lady seynte mary, and seynte petur and seynte poule, & alle holy halowes, apostelus, martyrres, conffessoures, virgines, & alle þe holy cu*m*pany of heuen, we denownce a-cursed, & owte of þe company of god & off alle holy chyrche de-parten, til þei come to amendmente.

¶ Inicientes manus violent*er* in presbit*erum* uel clericu*m*: extract*us* [2] de sentenc*iis*, Ca*pitulo*, *scilicet* .I°. c*apitulo*, p*er*uen*it*.

¶ Alle þat leyne hand on preste or clerke, or of man or womman lerud or lewode, off religione p*ro*fessed or vnp*ro*fessud, wit-in chirche or chirche-yarde, willynge in vyolens to do hym harme, & alle þ*at* þere-to p*ro*curron, or ȝeuon helpe or counsayle.

[1] *Lf.* 124.

[2] ? for 'extravagantes.'

¶ Infringentes libertates ecclesie.

¶ Alle þat brekon þe Franchyse & þe Fredam of holy chirche, And alle þat malyciouslye takuth or reuyth þe rythe, & bethe a-boute to lette or disturbul here Fredam *in* any wyse. ¶ Also alle þoo þat for wrathe or for hatte off any persone or vicare propur teyȝ-þingges wit-halduth, or distroyen wit hemself or wit here bestes, or beron a-way, & alle þat concente þer-to, in harmynge of þe person or off þe vicar, or off here procatoures. ¶ Also alle þoo þat Falsely, for malyce or for evolle wil, any person or vicar or preste, defame, or procureth to be famyd.

¶ Impetrans scienter literras ac falsas papales. Extractus de *Capitulo* ad falsarii, *scilicet* dura.

¶ Alle þat falsen þe popus selle or his[1] letteres, or þe kynges. ¶ And alle þat, be here wyttynge, purchasuth or maynteneth or vseth, or any þinge doþe þere-wyth be here wyttynge.

¶ In constitucionibus Johannis stratforde. *Capitulo* superno dei.

¶ Also alle þoo þat disturbulleth pes of holy chirche, or pes of þe lande. ¶ Also alle þat oþur statutes or lawes, or customes or vsages, areruth or makuth, or wryteth or holeuth, of holy churche, oþur þan[2] were wonte to bene. ¶ Alle þoo þat lettuth þe rytheful patron to present his chyrche þat he hathe ryte to, where-by he losuth [3]his presentatione at þat tyme.

¶ Extractus de sentenciis de *Capitulo* Noueritis.

¶ Also alle þat vnrytheffully settyth tallages vppon men of haly chirche, as podage, gwyage, or any oþur vnskylful thraldom, or warneth lewod men to selle hem owthe, or to bye of hem, or to grynde here corne or to bake here brede, or to do hem oþur seruice, & alle þat þer-to prokoron or helpon.

[1] MS. hit. [2] MS. þan; *e* altered to *a*. [3] *Lf.* 124 *bk.*

¶ Ex*tra*ct*us*[1] de sentenc*ii*s zos*imi*. *Capitulo* Quemq*uam*, li*br*o vj°, in constituc*ionibus* oxon*ie* p*a*pe Clement*is*, v*ersu*m de censura. *Capitulo* present*is*. *Capitulo* ext*ra*ct*us* de Nu*nc*. *Capitulo* eos qui, li*br*o vj°.

¶ Alle þat holy chyrch brenneth or robbuth, be nyȝte or be day, taky*ng* oute holy þinge or vnholy þing*e* vnskylfullyche.

¶ xj.j. in canone xvij.j.iiij. D*omi*nis .xxiij.j. vltinam pessimam.

¶ Also alle þoo þat purchason, in kyng*us* courte or in any oþur courte, wryttus or letteres or atthachement*es* to lette or disturbul p*ro*cesse or folowing of þe law, or of causes þ*at* ryȝtefully schulde be pursued in cryston courte, & be endud; eyþer wit strenȝþe or wit drede of boste, aferuth or lettuth any mynyster of holy chirche to do his office, and execuc*i*on of þing*e* þ*at* to hem longuth.

¶ In constitut*ione* octo-boni.

¶ Alle þ*at* howses or maneres, or any oþur places of any maner mann*us* of holy chyrche, any þyng takuth, reuyth, or doþe away, wit-oute leue of þe keper. ¶ Alle þ*at* draweth any man owte of holy chirche, or of cloystur, or off seyntwary, þ*at* is flowon þ*er*-to to haue grythe þere-off, þ*at* is, of holy chirch, & alle þ*at* þere-to helputh, in counsel or dede; & alle þ*at* lettuth here lyflode þe whyle þ*at* þei bene þ*er*-ine. ¶ Also alle þat brekuth or lettuth sequestracion of any p*re*latys, wit-oute here leue. ¶ Also alle þ*at* schaseth or hunteth men of holy chyrch, to make hem to syne here benefices a-ȝeynus here wille, or lettuth hem þ*at* bene synud to þe courte of rome, þ*at* þei no mowe go þidur in sauynge off þere ryȝthe; & alle þ*at* lettuth any man to purchase þe popus bullus or byschopp*us* letturres in defence of his rythe, and holy chyrche, & malyciously lettuth here processe.

¶ In constituc*ione* Joh*ann*is de stratforde. O. seculi p*r*incipes.

¶ Also alle þ*at* lettuth þe kynges heste to make hem, þei beþe

[1] ? for 'Extravagantes.'

acursud afftur fourety dayes to do hem to *pre*son, a*n*d do lyueraunce vnrythefully *pro*curuth, or þei be buxum to holy chyrche.

¶ In constitucione Joh*ann*is stradforde. O. quia diuin*us*.

¶ Also alle þ*at* distroyeth treus, gresse, wilfully, growinge in chirche-yarde, a-ȝeynus þe luff of hym þ*at* is kep*er* þer-off, þat is for to sayne, p*er*son or vicar. ¶ Also alle lewed men þ*at* enturmetuth hym off offeringus in chirche or in schapeƚƚ, [1] aȝeynus þe leue and fful wille of hym þ*at* hit longuth to. ¶ Also alle þ*at* disturbulleth pes of the londe, & alle felon*us* and may[*n*]teneres of Felonye. ¶ Also all traytoures, and alle comun thefu*us* & robberus ande houce-brenneres in tyme off pes, & falce conspirotoures, & alle falce-swerers in a-syse, be hem wyttynge, & alle false be-gynneres off false quereles, & helperes þer-to. ¶ Also alle okereres, and alle þ*at*, wit hem assentes & mayneteneth ȝefing*e*,[2] or takynge or sellyng þe darrer be-cause of lone. ¶ Also alle þ*at* makuth or wryteth statutes þ*at* okur schulde be payed, or ȝif þ*at* hit be payud, & be not restorud: alle þ*at* haue suche statutes, bot ȝif þai do hem a-way & distroy hem, þei ben a-cursud. ¶ Also alle þ*at* selle be falce mesoures, ellen yarde, galon or bussell, potelle or quarte, or be any falce wheytus, or selluth be one busselle, & buyuth be anoþ*ur*, & alle þ*at* suche vsith, be here wyttinge. ¶ Also alle þ*at*, for hate & for wynnynge, make men [3] to lose here catelle maliciouslye before any domus-man in willing of vengeaunce. Also alle þ*at* falcely w*ith*-holdes tythes rythefully longynge to holy chyrche, ouþur be wille or be wyttyng*e* ffalsely tythes, takyng to god þe worce, & hymself þe bettur, aȝeynus þe ordinawnce of Boniface, sum-tyme archebyschoppe of Caunturbery, þ*at* ordaynud thorowȝ alle þe archebyschopryche. ¶ "Hit is to tyȝe[4] of froyte, of corne, sede, herbys & gardynes, holly, wit-owte any lakkynge, or costus abbatinge. ¶ Off hey, where-sere hit growes, in grete mydowes or smale, as ofte os hit is y-mowe. ¶ Off noryssynge of alle maner of bestus, os of lombe, þe .vij., & so vpwarde, schal be

[1] *Lf.* 125.
[2] For 'þefinge,' thieving, see note 4.
[3] MS. make men make men.
[4] The use of ȝ for þ is seen also in some of the scraps in *Religious, Political, and Love Poems* (E.E.T. Soc., 1866), near the end.

taken in tyþe; and fro vj downewarde, for-ȝeueth one a halpeny, bot ȝif þe person or þe vicar vowche-saffe to a-byde tyl anoþur ȝere. ¶ Off mylk, alle þe whyle hit dureth, as wel in wyntur os in somur, or ellys gre þere-fore. ¶ Off fyssynge, of bene, of venison, & of oþur maner of goddus ryȝthefully I-wonne þat neweth be þe ȝere, as ofte os hit neweth. ¶ Also off profyte off mylnus, & werus & Fyssynge, no coste abatud, bot to þe selue valu schal be payed. ¶ Off lesowes, boþe comyn & seuerrelle, schal tyþe be payud trewly, aftur þe noumbur of þe bestus, oþur dayes, os hit is moste profyte in holy chirche. ¶ Also of coltus & caluus & pyggus, of gesse, off pychonus, of flax, of hempe, of corne, & of alle maner oþur þingus þat neweth be ȝere. ¶ Also of wolle-men, off schapmen, off wynnynge of þer crafte or schaffare; of carpenteres, off smythes, off webbys, brewerrus, & alle oþur men þat goth to hyre, & be þe weke, schal tyþe þe dole off þer hyre þat [1]he takuth, bot ȝif þei ȝiff any certeyne þere-fore to holy chirche at he[re] wille. ¶ Also of croppynge of treus, and of alle maner of vndurwode i-waxon & newode witine xx wyntur."

¶ In constitucione Iohannis stratforde. *Capitulo* quicq*uam* exsoluentur.

¶ Also alle þat falcely or be fraude teyþen here corne aftur þat hit be gadurred, & þat tyȝing steluth, or wylfullych, wit bestus or wit-owte, ellys destroyeth. ¶ And þei þat lettuth tyȝynge to be sette be skylful way. ¶ Also alle þat letton or with-holdon offeringe or custome skylful of deuocione vsud *in* owlde lawe tyme in any chirche, wo-sere hit be, & þer-to procuron. ¶ Also alle[2] eretekkes þat done wyttyngly aȝeynus þe lawe of criste & þe fayth of cristendome, in worde or in dede, oþur counsayle or ensampul ȝif, & alle þat fauereth hem in heresye. ¶ Also alle þat defamyth man or womman, where-thoroȝgh here state and here gode name is apeyrud, for envye or for hate. Also alle þat falsen þe kyngus money, or clypputh hit. ¶ Also alle þat ordenuth or beruth falce

[1] *Lf.* 125, back.
[2] MS. ¶ Also alle. ¶ Also alle.

wyttenesse aȝeynus matrimoyne lawfully made, or aȝeynus testament*us* þ*at* is trew be custome, wyttyngely. ¶ Also alle þ*at* helpon, or with strenkȝgh or wit vitayles, or sokoron, Iewus or sarsenus a-ȝeynus c*r*istendome. ¶ Also alle þ*at* slene childeron, or distroyen borne or vnborne, wyttyngly or wit wychecrafte, & alle here concentoures. ¶ Also alle þ*at* standuth & herkenyth be nytestyme vndur wowes, dorres, or wyndowes, for to a-spye towching euele, & alle houce-brekeres[1] and man-quelleres. ¶ Also alle þat comyn with [2]cursud men oþur wommen wykkydly, & alle þ*at* maynetenuth hem to here synne. ¶ Also alle þ*at* makuth false scharterus or false heyrus wyttyngliche. ¶ Also alle þ*at* makon exp*er*iment*us* or wyche-crafte, or charmys with coniurac*io*ns, & alle þ*at* leuon on hem. ¶ Also alle þ*at* defoylum holy chirche, or seyntwary or chir[che-] ȝarde,[3] where-þorogħ goddys seruice is note sayde nor done os hit felle for to be, til þei come to amendemente. ¶ Also alle þ*at* false executores þ*at* makon falce testamentes & wykkydly deserueth[4] þe godus of þe dedus, or do oþur þan þe wille of þe dedus was, & ful-fylleth note his queste to chirche or to any oþur place. ¶ Also alle þ*at* turneth fro crystendome to ethen-[5]nesse. ¶ Also alle þ*at* leuyn[6] here childur at any crosse or at any chyrche dorre, or any wayes, & leuyth hem þare.

Isto modo debet p*ro*nunciare centenciam:

¶ By þe auctorite of oure Fadur,[7] of þe sone of þe ħoly goste, & off ou[r]e lady seynte mary, goddus modur of heuen, and alle oþur virgynes, and seynte myhel, And alle oþur angellus and archangellus, And Petur and poule And oþur apostolus, and seynte

[1] See above, p. 63, l. 16.
[2] MS. comy cursud, as if repeating 'comyn.'
[3] See above, p. 64, l. 5, and p. 11, l. 330.
[4] ? unpreserves, steals; or an extension of sense, t. 4, *N.E.D.*, earn, win, and so get, take.
"I should rather translate it by 'inherit,' or 'take possession of, as if by inheritance.' Godefroy has: '*deserveor*, celui qui dessert ou régit* *un heritage*, une propriété.' It depends partly on the fact that *deserve* is often used in an ill sense: as to deserve death, deserve punishment, etc. See Cotgrave. But the particular sense of 'inherit' is the easiest to take."—W. W. SKEAT.
[5] *Lf.* 126.
[6] ? for 'lay in.'
[7] Father D.; *om.* C., which has 'Fadur' below.

* "seigniorizes over."—Cor.

stewne And alle oþur martyres, And seynte nicholas And alle oþur confessoures, And alle þe holy halowes of hewen,—we acurson, and waryon, And dep*ar*ton from alle gode dedus & prayeres of holy chyrche, and dampnon in-to þe peyne of helle, Alle þoo þ*at* haue done þeis articoles þ*at* we haue sayde before, tul þei comen to amendemente. ¶ We acurson hem be þe auctorite off þe courete off Rome, wit-inne and wit-oute forȝþe, sclepynge & wakynge, goynge, syttynge, and standi*n*ge, lyggynge of-bowne þe erthe & vndur þe erthe, spekynge, rydynge, [1] goynge, syttynge, stondynge,[1] etynge, drynkynge, in wode, in watur, in felde & in towne. ¶ We acurson be þe Fadur & sone & holygoste. A-cursyn hem angelus and archangellus, & alle þe nyne ordorus of heuen. A-cursyn hem patriarchus, p*ro*phetus, and apostolus, & alle goddus disciplus ; And alle holy innocentus, martyres, confessoures & virgynes, monkus, cannon*us*, eremytus, & prestus and clerkus, þ*at* þei haue no p*ar*te off masses ne mateyn*us* ne euensonge, ne of none oþur gode prayeres þ*at* bene done in holy chyrche, no in none oþ*ur* holy place, bot þe peynus of helle for to be here mede, wit Iudas þ*at* be-trayed oure lorde ih*es*u cryste, & þe lyf of hem be putte oute of þe bokus of lyfe, tyl þay comen to amendemente, & satisfaccion made. fiat, fiat! ame*n*!

¶ þan þou, þi candul, kaste to grownde,
Ande spytte þerto þe samë stownde,
And lette also þe bellë knylle,
to make hertus þe morë grylle.
oþ*ur* poynt*us* bene many & fele,
þ*at* be nót wel for to hele,
þ*at* þou myȝte know þi selfë beste,
in þe schartur of þe foreste ;
In þe grete chartur also
þou myȝte se many mo.

[1] These repetitions are in the MS.

SEVEN QUESTIONS TO BE ASKED OF A DYING MAN.

LANSDOWNE MS. 762, Fol. 21*b*.

Here folowethe vij specialle interrogacions The whiche a Curat aught to aske euery cristene persone that lieth*e* in the extremytie of deth*e*.

The first. Belevest thowe fully all*e* the pryncipall*e* articles of the Feith*e*, and also all*e* holy scripturs in all*e* thynge*s* after the exposicion*e* of the holy & trewe doctours of holy Chirch*e*, & forsakest all*e* heresies & arrours & opynyons dampned by the Chirch*e*? and arte glad also that thowe shalt dye in the feith*e* of Criste, & in the vnytie & obedience of holy Chirch*e*? The Sike p*er*son*e* answereth*e*, Yee.

Dost thou believe the principal articles of the faith and the holy Scriptures, and dost thou forsake heresy?

The second. knowest thowe, & knowligest thowe howe[1] thowe often*e* tymes & many man*er* wise & grevowsely thowe hast offended thy lorde god that made the of nought? for saint Barnard saith*e* vpon Cantica canticor*um*, "I knowe wele that there maye no man*ne* be saved but yef he knowe hym self." Of the whiche knowlage wexeth*e* a man*e* the Moder of his helth*e* that is humylitie, and also the drede of God, the whiche drede, as it is the begynnyng of wisdom*e*, So it is the begynnyng of mannys Soule? he answereth*e*, Yee.

[1 MS. nowe.]

Dost thou know that thou hast often offended God?

The thirde. Arte thowe sory in thy harte of all*e* man*er* of Synnys that thowe hast doon*e* ayenst the high*e* Magestie and the love and the goodnesse of God, & of all*e* goodnesse

Art thou sorry for thy sins?

that thowe hast not & myghtyst haue doone, & of alle graces that thowe hast forslowthed, not onely for drede of dethe

[*Fol. 22a.]

*or any other payne, but rather more for love of god & rightvsnesse, & for thowe hast displeased his grete goodnesse & kyndenesse, & for the due ordre & charitie by the whiche we be boundene to love god aboue alle thynge: & of alle thise thynges thowe askest forgevenes of god? desirest thowe also in thyne harte to haue very knowing of alle the offences that thowe hast doone ayenst god, and for to haue specialle repentaunce of theym alle? he answerethe, Yee.

and desirest to amend?

The Fourthe. Purposest thowe verely, & arte in fulle wille to amende the, & thowe myghtest live lenger, & neuer to Synne more dedely, wittyngly & with thy wille? & Rather thanne thowe woldest offende god dedely any more, to leve & lese wilfully alle erthly thynges, were they neuer so lefe to the, and also the life of thy body? and farthermore thowe prayest God, that he yeve the grace to contynue in this purpose? he answerethe, Yee.

Dost thou forgive thy enemies?

The Fifte. Foryevest thowe fully in thy harte alle maner of mene that euer haue the any harme or grevaunce vnto this tyme, other in worde or in dede, for the love & the worshipe of our lorde Ihesu criste, to whome thowe hopest to haue forgivenesse of thy selfe, & askest also thy self to haue forgivenesse of alle theym that thowe hast offended in any maner wise? he answerethe, Yee.

Art thou willing in all manner to make satisfaction?

The Sixte. Wolde thowe that alle maner thynges that thowe hast in any maner wise myght be fully restored ayeyne as moche as thowe mayest, & thowe arte bounde after the value of thy good, & rather leve & forsake alle thy good of the worlde, yef thowe mayest not make satisfaccione in none other wise? he answerethe, Yee.

Dost thou believe that Christ died for thee?

[*Fol. 22b.]

The Seventhe. Belevest thowe fully that Criste dyed *for the, and that thowe may neuer be saved but by the Merite of Cristes passione, and thanne thankest therof god with thyne harte asmoche as thowe mayest? he answerethe, Yee.

Than*ne* let the Curat desire the sike p*er*son*e* to saye 'In Manus tuas & *cetera*' with*e* a good stedfast mynde, and yf that he can*ne*; And yef he cannot, let the Curate saye it for hym, And who so eu*er* may verely, of very good consience & trowth*e* w*ith*out any faynyng, answere 'yee,' to all*e* the articles & poynt*es* afore Rehersed, he shall*e* live eu*er* in hevyn*e* w*ith* all*e* myghtie god and with*e* his holy Cvmpany; whervnto Ihe*s*us brynge both*e* yowe and me! Amen*e*!

The curate to cause the sick person to say "in manus tuas."

If he cannot say it the curate is to say it for him.

NOTES.

Page 1, line 5. *Dawe*, a form of Day. A.S. *Dæg*.

"Wel is us nu, Louerd, uor þe *dawes* þet tu lowudest us mide oðre monnes wouhwes."—*Ancren Riwle*, 190.

"Byuore Myhelmasse he was ycrouned þre *dawes* & nan mo."—*Rob. of Glouc.* 383.

"Suche mawmetys he hade yn hys *dawe*."—*Constitutions of Masonry*, p. 31, l. 509.

Done of Dawes = taken from day = killed.

"And alle *done of dawez* with dynttez of swreddez."—*Morte Arthure* (ed. Perry), p. 61, l. 2056.

"ȝyf þou do any man o *dawe*."—*Rob. of Brunne, Handlynge Synne*, p. 34, l. 1034.

Is glossed "to the deþ."

The seventeenth century phrase, "done to death," is an echo of the older idiom.

l. 11. *Preste curatoure* = Priest who has cure of souls. These directions are only meant for such as have to take part in active ministrations; they relate to the priest's duties to a flock, not to the church, or his own soul.

P. 2, l. 23. The chastity here meant includes not only abstinence *ab illicitis*, but also from wedlock. When this treatise was written, the Church in England had long refused its sanction to the marriage of persons in holy orders. Though it was contrary to the theory of the Western Church from very early days, there is the most positive evidence that before the Norman Conquest English priests were frequently married. In the North of England celibacy was the exception rather than the rule. A clerical family, whose pedigree has been compiled by Mr. Raine (*Priory of Hexham*, Surtees Soc., v. i. p. li.), held the office of Priest of Hexham from father to son for several generations. Priests' children constantly occur in mediæval records; *e.g.*, in William Painell's conformation charter to the nuns of Gokewell (The Well of the Cuckoo) executed within a century of the Conquest, mention is made of "unum molendinum quod fuit Rodberti filii presbiteri" (*Linc. Arch. Soc. Rep.*, 1854, p. 102). The decrees of provincial councils show that priestly concubinage was in practice down to the period of the Reformation. The issue of such unions must have been sufficiently numerous to attract attention, for we find in 1281 the constitutions of Archbishop Peckham providing that priests' children should not succeed to their father's benefices, "absque dispensatione apostolica" (Wilkins, *Conc.* ii. 60). Strange things are told of dispensations, yet some will hardly believe Rycharde Layton, when he says of Jenyn, the last Prior of Maiden Bradley in Wiltshire, that, "The pope, consideryng his fragilitie, gave him licens to kepe an hore, and [that he] hath goode writyng *sub plumbo* to discharge his conscience" (*Letters on Suppression of Monast.*, Camd. Soc., p. 58). The tale is not incredible, but it comes from one whose words have slender authority. If the story be true, it speaks ill for the persons who were then ruling in matters spiritual, for Jenyn, after the suppression of his house, became rector of Shipton Moyne, co. Gloucester.

l. 31. *Dronkelec*, Dronkelewe. Drunkenness. A MS. of the 15th cent. (Add. 12,195) bids folk take care that a nurse "be wysse and well a-vyssyd, and þat sche lof þe chylde, and þat sche be not *dronkeleche*." — *Prompt. Par.* i. 133. A piece of advice which is, I am informed, not entirely unneeded in these days. As to the termination *lac*, see Cockayne's *Seinte Marherete*, 101.

l. 43. *Pyked schone* came into use in the reign of William Rufus. It is said that the world owes this silly fashion to the ingenuity of Fulk, Earl of Anjou, who had deformed feet, and sought by this strange device to hide the defect from view. The pikes were sometimes made like the tails of scorpions, at others twisted into the form of a ram's horn. At a later period these long-toed boots were called cracowes from the belief that they were originally imported from Cracow. In Mr. C. R. Smith's collection of London Antiquities, now in the British Museum, are some shoes of this sort of the era of Edward IV.; the toes are six inches long and stuffed with moss. A long-toed patten was introduced for the use of persons who delighted in these fantastic habiliments. I presume this is alluded to in the *Detecta quædam in visitat. Eccl. Cath. Ebor.*, A.D. 1390, where it is stated that "Omnes ministri Ecclesiæ pro majori parte, utuntur in Ecclesia et in processione *patens* et *clogges* contra honestatem Ecclesiæ et antiquam consuetudinem et ordinacionem capituli."—*Surtees Soc.* 35, p. 243. The use of shoes of this sort was prohibited to the clergy by many local councils. See Du Frene, *Gloss. sub voc. Pigaciæ et Rostra.* Constitutions of London, A.D. 1342, in Wilkin's *Conc.* ii. 703. Fairholt's *Satirical Songs on Costume*, 43. Hewitt's *Ancient Armour*, i. 136.

l. 48. *Baselard.* A short sword worn by civilians in the fourteenth and fifteenth centuries. It is frequently shown on monumental effigies. A brass at King's Sombourne, co. Hants., where one is represented, is engraved in Hewitt's *Ancient Armour and Weapons*, ii. 254.—*Gent. Mag.* 1858, ii. 559. The Baselard was of two kinds—straight and curved. It was one of the former kind that Sir William Walworth presented to the Fishmongers' Company. The hooked or curved baselard was an Eastern weapon (*Prompt. Par.* i. 25). Capgrave tells us that Edmond Ironside was "slayn be the councel of Edrede, the duke; for he mad his son for to hide him undir a sege, where the King shuld voide, and sodeynly with a scharp *basulard* he smet the Kyng among the boweles."—*Chron.*, 125. By Statute 12, Richard II. c. vi. it was provided that, "null servant de husbandrie ou laborer ne servant de artificer ne de vitailler ne porte desore enavant *baslard*, dagger, nespee sur forfaiture dicelle." Priests were strictly inhibited from wearing this instrument of war, but the rule was constantly broken.

> "Bucklers brode, & swerdes long,
> Baudrike, with *baselardes* kene,
> Soch toles about her necke they hong:
> With Antichrist soche priestes been."
>
> *Plowman's Tale*, part 3.

That ordinances against the clergy wearing secular arms were not needless, is evident from many incidental notices in our records. On the 5th October, 1509, the Jury of the Manor of Kirton in Lindsey presented that "Hugo Colynson capellanus vi & armis [*fecit*] affr*aiam* sup*er* Will*ielmo* ffrema*n* & violent*er* extraxit sanguinem contra pace*m* d*omi*ni regis." On the 22nd February, 1515, the same body, "dicunt q*uod* Will*ielmus* Brown Cl*er*icus p*ar*ochialis de Kytton vi & armis fec*it* affr*aiam* sup*er* Will*ielmo* Wilkynson de Wadyngham" (*Rot. Cur.*). A satirical song of the early part of the 15th century, beginning—

> "Prenegard, prenegard, thus bere I myn *baselard*,"

is printed in Fairholt's *Satirical Songs on Costume*, Percy Soc., p. 50.

l. 48. *Bawdryke.* Lat. *Baldrellus, Baldringus Baltheus.* French, *Baudrier.* A girdle or belt of any sort. It is used here for the sword-belt, probably for one of that kind that hangs over the right shoulder, and passes transversely across back and breast.

> "Then þay schewed hym þe schelde, þat was of schyr goulez,
> Wyth þe pentangel de-paynt of pure golde hewez;
> He braydez hit by þe *baude-ryk*, a-boute þe hals kestes
> Þat bisemed þe segge semlyly fayre."
>
> *Sir Gawayne and the Green Knight*, p. 20, l. 621.

The *Baudrick* or *Baldryck* of a church bell was the whitleather thong, by which the clapper was suspended from the eye or staple in the crown of the bell. The word is of constant occurrence in old churchwardens' accounts.

[1428] Sol*uti* Thom*æ* Basse p*ro* j baudryk vj*d.*

Ch. Acc. St. Mary, Stamford, Cotton MS. Vesp. A. 24, f, 3, b.

[1498] "Payd to John Clarke for makyng of a *bawdre* to ye bell, 1*d.*"

[1502] "Payd to John Dalbe for *bavdrec* makyng to þe bell*es*, vi*d.*"

Ch. Acc., Leverton, Co. Linc., MS. fol. 6, 8.

[15 . .] "Paid for makyng of a belle *batrey* and mending, viij*d.*"

[1535] "Payd to roger codder for iij *bautres* making vi*d.*"

Ch. Acc., Kirton in Lindsey, MS. p. 14, 19.

l. 49. For illustrations of the history of the clerical tonsure consult Bingham, *Antiq. Christ. Church*, b. vj. c. iv. Rock, *Ch. of our Fathers*, v. i. p. 185. Lyndwood, *Provinciale*, lib. i. tit. 14, p. 69. Beda, *Eccl. Hist.* lib. v. c. xxi. Beyerlinck, *Magnum Theatrum Vitæ Humanæ*, sub voc. *Tonsura.* Martene, *De Antiq. Eccl. Rit.* (Venetiis, 1783), vol. ii. p. 14; vol. iii. p. 284, 293, 300, 335; vol. iv. p. 113, 174, 238, 274.

P. 3, l. 59. *Schrewes.* In the older English this word stands for enemies, wretches, or evil-disposed persons of either sex.

> "Þe Cristene men leyde euere on, & slowe euere to grounde,
> Al clene þe *ssrewen* were ouercome in a stounde."
>
> "He adde endyng, as he wurþe was, & such yt ys to be a *ssrewe.*"
> *Rob. Glouc.* 407, 419.
>
> "Such qualité nath noman to beo lechour other *schrewe.*"
> *Pop. Treatises on Science*, p. 133.

l. 82. *Hosele*, to administer the holy communion, A.S. *Husl*, an offering, an oblation, and hence the host, as the highest of all offerings. To housel was the ordinary name for the act of giving the communion until the period of the Reformation. From the earliest times, as far as we know, in this country the altar breads were in the form of wafers—thin and round cakes stamped with some sacred device or monogram. That they differed from the coarse household bread of the people is indicated by the fact that the sons of Sabert (Sœberht), the Christian king of the East Saxons, *circa* 604, who had remained out of the Christian fold, when they asked Bishop Melitus, after their father's death, why he would not give them the eucharist of which he had been accustomed to partake, said, as we have their words reported to us in Latin, "quare non et nobis porrigis panem nitidum, quem et patri nostro dabas."—Beda, *Hist. Eccl.* lib. ii. c. 5.—These altar breads were frequently called *obleys.* Lat. *oblata.* It is believed that they were usually made by nuns, or anchoresses. It was so certainly in the ninth century in France. There is a tale told in a contemporary life of St. Wandragesilius, Abbot of Fontenelle, a Benedictine monastery on the Seine, near Rouen, of a certain nun who went to the fire for the purpose of baking this bread, holding in her hand the iron stamps for the purpose. "Accessit ad ignem, ferroque quo imprimendæ ac decoquendæ erant oblatæ, arrepto, mox nervi manus ejus dexteræ contracti sunt, ac oblatorium quod sponte susceperat, invita, vi agente divina retinuit."—*Acta Sanct. Julii*, t. v. p. 290, n. 53. As quoted in Rock, *Ch. of our Fathers*, v. i. p. 152.

The altar breads were of two kinds. The larger, called singing-bread, were used for the sacrifice; the smaller, called houseling-bread, were used for the communion of the people. They were sometimes kept for sale by country shopkeepers (*Gent. Mag.* 1864, pt. ii.

p. 502). There is preserved in the Rotuli Parliamentorum, 1472-3, a curious petition from Johanna Glyn, widow of John Glyn, of Morvale, in the county of Cornwall, gentleman, in which she complains of the bad treatment her late husband had received from the hands of certain rioters. Among other things she says, "The said Riottours, the same day and place toke the said John Glyn and hym ymprisoned, and in the Castell, in prisone hym kept by the space of v oures, and more, so that noon of his frendes myght come where he was to releve hym with drynk, or staunche his bloode, to th'entent that he shuld have bled to deth, except they suffered a Preste to come to shryve and *howsell* hym."—Vol. vj. p. 35.

In the *Privy Purse expences of Henry viij.* are several entries similar to the following, the interpretation of which has been held to present a difficulty:—"I*tem* the x daye [of April, 1530] paied to maist*er* Weston by way of the king*es* rewarde ayenst easter, xx*s*." "I*tem* the same daye, paied by lyke rewarde to the two guilliams and phillippes boye for ther *howsell*, x*s*. a pece, xxx*s*."—p. 38, *cf.* 40, 41, 330. There can be no doubt that the meaning is, that the king presented to the persons named x*s*. for them to give as an offering at their Easter communion.

The little bell, which it was the practice to ring before the holy eucharist when the priest took it to the sick, was called a *howslinge* bell. See Peacock's *Eng. Church Furniture*, p. 86. Housel-sippings was the unconsecrated wine which was given at certain times to the lay folk out of the chalice. Bishop John Bale says, "They will pay no more money for the *housel*-sippings, bottom blessings, nor for seyst me and seyst me not above the head and under of their chalices."—*Image of both Churches*, edit. 1849, p. 526.

A *houseling-towel* or *houseling-cloth* was the linen sheet used when the holy communion was received for the purpose of hindering particles thereof from falling on the ground. "A *howslyng* tewell, off dyaper, w*ith* blew melyngs atte the ende, goode."—*Ch. Goods, St. Dunstan's Canterbury. Gent. Mag.*, 1837, pt. 2, p. 570. A cloth of this kind was employed at royal coronations until recent times. That of William IV. was the first where it was disused.—Maskell, *Mon. Rit.* iii. 834.

l. 87. Midwives were licensed by the bishop of the diocese. These licences continued to be issued till long after the Reformation. The form may be seen in Strype's *Annals*, vol. i. p. 242. In Grindal's *Articles to be enquired into in the Province of Canterbury*, A.D. 1576, the fifty-eighth question is, "Whether there be any among you that use sorcery, or witchcraft, or that be suspected of the same, and whether any use any charmes or unlawful prayers, or invocations in Latin or otherwise, and, namely, midwives in the time of woman's travail of child, and whether any do resort to any such help or counsel, and what be their names."—Grindal's *Remains*, p. 174.

In Bale's *Comedye concerninge thre Lawes*, 1528, sig. B. iii. b., as quoted in Brande's *Pop. Antiq.*, 1813, v. ii. p. 5, we have a notice of some of the superstitious doings of midwives.

> "Yea, but now ych am a she,
> And a good mydwyfe perde,
> Yonge chyldren can I charme,
> With whysperynges and whysshynges,
> With crossynges and with kyssynges,
> With blasynges and with blessynges,
> That spretes do them no harm."

Midwives sometimes murdered children for purposes of magic. Sprenger, in his *Malleus Malificarum*, v. 2, as quoted in Beyerlinck, *Mag. Theat. Vitæ Humanæ*, v. vij. p. 784, b., tells us of the burning of two women of this class, "quia earum vna quadraginta altera innumerabiles pueros recens in lucem editos necavissent, inditis clam in eorum capita grandibus aciculis."

P. 4, l. 95. De baptismo infantium, quos mater in partu laborans, in lucem emitterè non valet, ita definiunt antiqua Statuta Synodalia Ecclesiæ Nemausiensis [Nismes] . . . . Si vero, muliere in partu laborante, infans extra ventrem matris caput tantum emiserit, et in tanto periculo infans positus nasci nequiverit, infundant aliqua de obstetricibus aquam super caput infantis dicens, 'Ego baptizo te in nomine Patris,' etc., et erit baptizatus. His concinunt Statuta Synodalia ecclesiæ Biterrensis a Guillelmo episcopo anno 1342 edita . . . . ab hac sententia non nihil deflectunt Statuta antiqua ecclesiæ Ruthensis. Sic enim habent capite sexto: Si vero, muliere in partu laborante infans extra ventrem matris caput tantum emiserit, et in tanto periculo infans positus commode haberi nequiverit, infundet aliquis vel aliqua de astantibus aquam super caput infantis, dicens: 'Creatura Dei, ego te baptizo in nomine Patris, & Filii, & Spiritus sancti.' Et erit baptizatus."—Martene, *De Antiq. Eccl. Rit.* i. 58, 59, where much more relating to this subject may be seen.

In the consistorial acts of the Diocese of Rochester, the following document relative to the baptism of a child during birth is preserved. I quote from the *Gentleman's Mag.* 1785, pt. ii. p. 939.

"1523, Oct. 14. Eliz*abeth* Gaynsford obstetrix examinat*a* dicit in vim juramenti sui sub hâc formâ verborum. I, the aforesaid Elizabeth, seeing the childe of Tho*mas* Everey, late born in jeapardy of life, by the authorite of my office, then beyng midwife, dyd christen the same childe under this manner, In the name of the Fader, the Son, and the Holy Ghost, I christen thee, Denys, iffundend*am* meram aquam super caput infantuli. Interrogata erat, Whether the childe was born and delivered from the wyfe of the said Thomas? Whereto she answereth and saith, that the childe was not born, for she saw nothyng of the childe but the hedde; and for the perell the childe was in, and in that tyme of nede, she christened [it] as is aforesaid, and cast water with her hand on the childes hede. After which so done, the childe was born, and was had to the churche, where the Priest gave to it that chrystynden that lakkyd, and the childe is yet alyf."

l. 116. In cases of necessity it was permitted to baptize in a wooden vessel, which was to be burned when the ceremony was over, to prevent its being used for secular purposes hereafter.—Martene, *De Antiq. Eccl. Rit.* i. 5.

l. 120. *Nuye*, Annoy, trouble. Old Fr. *Anoi* from Lat. *Odium.*

"And a ryche man hyt *noyeþ* oftyn tyde
Þat a pore man hat oghte besyde."

Rob. of Brunne, Handlynge Synne, p. 187, l. 5981.

P. 5, l. 133. *On rowe*, in order. A.S. *Rawa.*

"He rehersed be *rowe* the rite of Edgare."

Capgrave, *Chron.* 172.

The gild of St. Mary of Boston had, in 1534, a corporal, which was in part made of "*rawed* satten of brigges," *i.e.* Bruges satin made in rows or stripes. The editor's *Church Furniture*, p. 205. Lincolnshire people still speak of Turnip *raws.*

l. 143. Fonts were usually only blessed at Easter and Whitsuntide. When the service of blessing was performed they were vested in a linen cloth.—Martene, *De Antiq. Eccl. Rit.* iii. 150. Maskell, *Mon. Rit.* i. 13, where the service may be found.

l. 153. See exhortation in the Salisbury *Ordo ad faciendum Catechumenum.*—Maskell, *Mon. Rit.* i. 14. On the font at Bradley, co. Lincoln, is inscribed, "Pater noster ave maria and criede leren ye chyld yt es nede." The inscription is coeval with the font, *i.e.* circa A.D. 1500.

l. 153. "Inhibemus sub poena excommunicationis, ne aliquae mulieres vel uxores parvulos suos in lectulis suis secum collocari permittant, antequam ætatis suæ tertium annum impleverint. Quod statutum ad minus semel in anno singulis sacerdotibus volumus promulgari."—*Constitutiones synodales Sodorenses*, A.D. 1291. Cap. xiv. in Wilkins' *Conc.* ii. 177.

P. 7, l. 203. "Debet enim sacerdos *banna* in facie ecclesiæ infra missarum solemnia cum major populi adfuerit multitudo, per tres dies solemnes et disjunctas interrogare: ita ut inter unumquemque diem solemnem cadat ad minus una dies ferialis. Rubric in *Ordo ad faciendum Sponsalia.*"—Maskell, *Mon. Rit.* i. 44. In Lincolnshire the *banns* of marriage are called 'spurrings,' *i.e.* askings, from *Spere*, to enquire; A.S. *Spyrian*, to track; Dutch, *Speuren*; Germ. *Spuren.*

In the ancient office the earlier part of the rite took place "ante ostium ecclesiæ, coram Deo sacerdote et populo."

"Husbonds at chirche dore have I had fiue,
For I so often haue I-wedded be."

Chaucer, *Wife of Bath, Prolog.*

Martene has published from an ancient manual of the diocese of

Rheims the following verses, to aid in calling to mind the different hindrances to wedlock:

> "Error, conditio, votum, cognatio, crimen,
> Cultus, disparitas, ordo, ligamen, honestas,
> Si sis affinis, sique coiere nequis."
> *De Antiq. Eccl. Rit.* ii. 137.

P. 8, l. 241. It was in the Middle Ages, as at present, a matter of obligation for all Catholics to receive the holy communion at Easter-tide.

l. 247. *Ded*, death, a common provincialism. A Lincolnshire woman told the editor that she "would rather be nibbled to *dead* with ducks than live with Miss——; she is always a nattering."

l. 252. After communion it was the custom for the laity to drink unconsecrated wine, to assist them in swallowing the eucharistic wafer. The purchase of wine for this use sometimes appears in old accounts, and has led to the mistaken notion that it was a common practice in those days to give the communion in both kinds. The following passage from the account rolls of Coldingham is peculiarly liable to this misconstruction. 1364. "In vino empto per annum pro celebracione et pro communione parochianorum ad Pascham xv$^{s.}$ i$^{d.}$"—p. xliv, as quoted in Rock's *Ch. of our Fathers*, iii. pt. 2, p. 170. In the constitutions of Archbishop Peckham, promulgated in 1281, this practice is described in words, of which the text is a simple translation. "Doceant [sacerdotes] etiam eosdem illud, quod ipsis eisdem temporibus in calice propinatur, sacramentum non esse, sed vinum purum eis hauriendum, traditum, ut facilius sacrum corpus glutiant quod perceperunt."—Wilkins, *Conc.* ii. 52. It was ordained by the Synod of Exeter, A.D. 1287, that there should be in every church as well as the chalice employed in saying mass, a cup of silver or tin to be used when communion was given to the sick. In this cup the priest washed his fingers, and the sick man, after he had communicated, drank the water.—*Ibid.* ii. 139. The "device for the coronation of King Henry vij." published among the Rutland Papers (Camd. Soc.), p. 22, shows that he and his queen partook of a chalice of this kind at that high ceremony.

P. 9, l. 260. *Sad*, gravely. "He [Maurice, Lord Berkeley, born 1457] was called by writ to the state of a Baron, and recommended to provide a *sadd* gentlewoman in Court to wait upon my lady."—Forbroke's *Smith's Lives of the Berkeleys*, 175.

"But ye . . . vse . . . to loke so *sadly* wha*n* ye mene merely yt many times me*n* dowbte whyther ye speke in Sporte wha*n* ye mene good ernest."—*Sir Th. More, Workes*, 1557, p. 127 *b*.

l. 267. *Bordes*, Jests, games; Fr. *Bourde*; Dutch, *Boerde*; Lat. *Burdare*, to jest.

> "And y shal telle as y kan,
> A *bourde* of an holy man."
> *R. of Brunne, Handlyng Synne*, p. 287, l. 9260.

"We have so mocked him with his gospel that we shall find it is no *bourding* with him."—*John Bradford's Works*, v. i. p. 38.

"*Bourd* not wi' bawtie."—Scottish proverb, Ramsay's *Reminiscences of Scottish Life*, ii. edit. 139.

"The sooth *bourd* is nae *bourd*."—Scottish proverb, *Redgauntlet*, ch. xi.

l. 270. We have evidence here that at the time this poem was written, it was not a common thing for people to sit on benches in church. Nearly all the pre-Reformation church seats in existence in this country are of the late Perpendicular era. Pews were, however, in common use before the Reformation. Sir Thomas More frequently makes mention of them in such a manner as to show that they were no novelties to him. He tells us "how men fell at varyance for kissing of the pax, or goyng before in processi*on*, or setti*n*g of their wiues pewes in the church." We may surmise from this that pews were sometimes restricted to women. A pew seems, from the following story, to have been the eminence upon which offenders did public penance. "These witnes in dede will not lye; As the pore man sayd by the priest, if I may be homely to tell you a mery tale by the way. A mery tale, quod I, commith neuer amyse to me. The pore man, quod he, had founde ye priest ouer famyliar with his wife, and bycause he spake of it a-brode and coulde not proue it, the priest sued him before ye bishoppes offyciall for dyffamatyon where the pore man, vpon paine of cursynge, was commau*n*ded that in his paryshe chyrche, he should upon ye sondaye, at high masse time sta*n*de vp & sai, 'mouth, thou lyest.' Wherupo*n* for fulfilling of hys pena*n*ce, vp was the pore soule set in a pew, that ye peple might wo*n*der on him and hyre what he sayd. And there all a-lowed (whan he had rehersyd what he had reportyd by the priest) than he sett hes handys on his mouth and said, 'mouth! mouth, thou lyest.' And by and by therupon he set his hand vpon both his eyen & sayd, 'but eyen, eyen,' q*uod* he, 'by y^e^ mass ye lie not a whitte.'"—pp. 88, *c*. 127, *d*.

l. 272. In Durham *sitting on the knees* is an expression still used for kneeling.

l. 273. *Flat* = Floor.

"A hep of girles sittende aboute the *flet*."
Wright's *Political Songs*, Camd. Soc. p. 337.

The floors of the houses in Edinburgh, where each floor is the home of a separate family, are called *flats*. Houses containing only one family as occupants are known as "houses within themselves." See Scott's *Guy Mannering*, xxxvi. The warp on each side of the River Trent, that is, submerged by the tide, is called The Trent *Flat*. On the Lincolnshire coast, the low land on the shore is often named the *Flat*, as Sand Hall *Flat*, near Tetney Haven, and Friskney *Flat*.

l. 280. *Blesse*. That is, make the sign of the cross. This act is still called blessing one's-self by Catholics.

"The Apostles and Fathers of the Primitive Church blessed themselves with the sign of the cross."—John Marshall, as quoted by Fulke. Fulke's Works (Parker Soc.), ii. 171.

"Blest themselves with both hands" is Sir Thomas Urquhart's version of "se signoient, de toutes mains."—Rabelais, *Gargantua*, *b.* 1, c. xxxv.

l. 281. The versicle said immediately before the Gospel, in the Ancient English as in the Roman Mass, is, *Gloria tibi, Domine.*

l. 284. The sanctus sance or sauce bell was a small bell usually hung outside the church in a little hutch or cote on the east gable of the nave. This was rung at the elevation of the host in the parish mass, to warn all those who were not present at the service to join their hearts with the devotions of the worshippers. The sacring bell was a smaller bell of this kind, to be rung at other masses. It was sometimes hung in the rood loft; more commonly it was, as it is at present in Roman Catholic churches, merely a handbell. Handbells and sacring bells were among the things ordered to "be utterly defaced, rent, and abolished," in 1576.—Grindal's *Remains*, p. 159. They were mostly destroyed in Lincolnshire in or before A.D. 1566. See editor's *Church Furniture*, passim.

P. 10, l. 309. "Cum autem ad infirmum eucharistia deportatur, ita decenter se habeant portatores, superpelliciis saltem induti, cum campanella, lumine præcedente, nisi vel aëris intemperies obstet vel loci remotio; ut per hoc devotio fidelium augeatur, qui Salvatorem suum tenentur in via, luto non obstante, flexis genibus adorare, ad quod sunt per sacerdotes suos attentius commonendi."—W. de Cantilupe, *Constit.* A.D. 1240. In Wilkins' *Conc.* i. 667.

l. 315. After long search I have failed to find any passage similar to this in the writings of Augustinus. I am informed by two persons, who have made the writings of this saint an object of especial study, that no such statements occur in them.

P. 11, l. 330. *Seyntwary*, churchyard. The name of sanctuary is now given to that part of the choir or chancel of a church where the altar stands. In mediæval documents belonging to this country, *Sanctuarium* and its equivalents in English almost always mean churchyard. "Ecclesiarum *Sanctuaria*, quæ populariter coemeteria nominantur."—*Stat. Cicest.* in Wilkins' *Conc.* ii. 183. *Chirch hay*, churchyard. A.S. *Cyrce*, church, *Heg*, hay, grass, or *Hege*, a hedge, or fence.

l. 332. Games and secular business were forbidden in churchyards by the Synod of Exeter, A.D. 1287. Wilkins, *Conc.* ii. 140. By 12 Ric. II. c. vi. servants were ordered to amuse themselves with bows and arrows on Sundays, and to give up foot-ball, quoits, casting the stone, 'keyles,' and other such inopportune games. In consequence of this statute the jury of the manor of Kirton in Lindsey, 4th April, 1 Henry VIII., made a presentment that "Will*iel*m*us* Welton se male gessit in ludend*o* ad pilam pedalem et alia joca illicita."—*Rot. Cur.*

l. 332, note. *Stoil ball*, stool-ball. This game is still played in Sussex. There is a description of it in *Notes and Queries*, iii. s. xi. 457.

l. 338. The holding of fairs and markets in churchyards was made illegal by statute in 1285.—*Stat. Winhest.* 13 *Edw.* I. c. vj. The practice, however, of using churches and churchyards for secular purposes continued to be common. Edward I. received the oaths of the competitors for the Crown of Scotland in Norham Church. In 1326 the tythe corn of Fenham, Fenwick, and Beele was collected in the chapel at Fenham, and at about the same period, when the monks of Holy Island found their grange would hold no more, they converted the chapel attached to their mance into a temporary tythe barn.—Raine's *North Durham*, 82, 263. Law Courts were held, books sold, and children taught in the porch of St. Peter's, Sandwich.—Boys' *Hist. Sandw.* 365. A manor court, called Temple court, was held in the church of St. Mary, and St. John Baptist, Dunwich, annually on the feast of All Souls.—Gardner's *Dunwich*, 54. Wool was stored in one of the churches at Southampton.—J. T. Rogers, *Hist. of Agriculture*, i. 32; ii. 611; and a lawsuit settled in St. Peter's Church, Bristol.—Fosbroke's *Smith's Lives of the Berkeleys*, 92. In 1519 Pedlars were accustomed, on feast days, to sell their wares in the church porch of Ricall, co. York.—*Surtees Soc.* 35, p. 271.

l. 338. *Chost.* A.S. *Ceást*, strife.

> "& mad tille him feaute, withouten any *chest*,
> & cleymed him for þer chefe of West & of Est."
>
> *Langtoft Chron.* 19.

l. 353. Old Norse, *Naut*, an ox. A.S. *Nyten*, an animal, from *nitan* (*ne witan*), not to know. Scotch, *Nolt*.

P. 12, l. 358. *Fonne*, a fool. *Fond* = foolish is a Lincolnshire provincialism.

l. 360. *Telyng* means, as I conceive, rhythmical couplets or verses intended to charm away evil or cause good luck.

l. 366. *Gart*, third pers. sing. of *Gare*, to cause. O.N. *göra, gera*. A.S. *Gearwian*. Mod. Scotch, *Gar*.

> "My precios perle dotȝ me gret pyne,
> What serueȝ tresor, bot gareȝ men grete."
>
> *Allit. Poems*, E.E.T.S., p. 11, l. 330.

The following inscription wrought in stained glass once decorated a window in the church of Blyton, co. Linc.:

"Prieȝ for ye gild of Corpus Xpi quilk yis window garte mak."
Harl. MS. 6829, f. 198.

A mediæval bell still hangs in the church tower of Alkborough, a little Lincolnshire village near the point where the Trent falls into the Humber, on which is inscribed + Jesu : for : yi : modir : sake : save : al : the : savls : that : me : gart : make : amen.

l. 368. The following charm is worth reprinting here, as it occurs in a book where no one would think of looking for it. Hooper, the

Reformer, says that he knew a poor man who had it in his possession, vainly hoping that it could heal all diseases.

+ Jesus + Job + habuit + vermes + Job + patitur + vermes + in + nomine + Patris + et + Filii + et + Spiritus Sancti + amen + lama + ȝabacthani + .—*Early Writings*, Parker Soc. 328.

l. 372. *Okere*. usury. A.S. *Eácan*, to augment. Old Norse, *Okr*. Goth. *Aukan*. Usury has been a subject for much angry and protracted discussion. See Lecky's *Hist. Rationalism*, j. *passim*. The *Catechism of the Council of Trent* says, "Whatever is received above the principal, be it money, or anything else that may be purchased by money, is usury."—Pt. iij. chap. viij. quest xj., Donovan's *Transl.* Grindal's *Injunctions* of 1571 class usurers with "adulterers, fornicators, incestuous persons," and other like notorious criminals. They define usurers to be "all those who lend money, corn, ware, or other thing, and receive gain therefore over and above that which is lent."—*Remains*, 143. The imaginative literature of former times contains many stories of the unhappy fate of usurers. See for a copious collection of them, Beyerlinck, *Mag. Theat. Vitæ Humanæ*, v. vij. p. 1064.

In 1644 the churchwardens of Kirton in Lindsey put out money at eight per cent.; they note among their receipts, "Will*ia*m Kent, gen*tle*man, for 5 li vpon a bond 8*s*."—*Church Accounts, MS.* 197.

P. 13, l. 394. *Blyue*, quickly.

"Heo hadde þe maistry of þe feld, þe Romaynes flow *blyue*."
Rob. Glouc. p. 50 n.

"The kyng issued fro his navee *bliue*."
Romans of Partenay, p. 195, l. 5673.

l. 411. *Steuene*, voice. A.S. *Stefen*.

"Whan Litle John heard his master speake,
Well knew he it was his *steven*."
Robin Hood and Guy of Gisb. l. 210.

l. 419. *Gult*, trespass, guilt.

"Forȝif us our *gultes*, also we forȝifet oure gultare."
Maskell, *Mon. Rit.* ij. 238.

l. 420. *Fondynge*. A.S. *Fandian*, to try.

"Leod us in tol na *fandinge*."
MS. *Cot. Cleop.* B. vj. f. 201 in Maskell, *Mon. Rit.* ij. 238.

"Lat us nouȝt be *fonded* in sinne."
MS. *Bibl. Reg.* 5 c. v. as above, ij. 239.

P. 14, l. 422. The "Hail Mary," as at present used by Roman Catholics, was unknown in mediæval England. I believe the Sarum Breviary of 1531 is the earliest authority for the modern form. The Salisbury Primer of 1556 breaks off at the same point as the prayer in the text. Dr. Rock gives a most interesting dissertation on this prayer in his *Church of our Fathers*, iii. pt. i. p. 315.

P. 14, l. 426. In the 76th Catalogue of Albert Sutton, 8, Deansgate, Manchester, is the following entry:—"364 Lancashire.—White (John, Minister of God's Word at Eccles). The Way to the True Church, etc.; thick folio, calf, £1 1*s*. 1624. In the preface occurs the following bit of Lancashire folklore, which the author has labelled in the margin, 'The maner how the vulgar sort of people say their praiers':—

THE LITTLE CREED.

Little creed can I need,
Kneel before our Ladies knee:
Candles light, candles burne,
Our Lady prayed to her deare Sonne
That we might all to heaven come,
Little creed, Amen.

There are many other curious prayers, some in the Lancashire dialect. This copy contains 'The Orthodox Faith and way to the Church,' by Francis White, elder brother to Doctor John White."

P. 16, l. 499. *Dele*, Part. A.S. *Dǽl*, Part. Sansc. *Dal*, to split; hence, *Deal* and *Dole*, to distribute. *Deal*, a plank or separated piece of wood. *Deal*, at cards. *Dole*, money, food, or raiment given by way of alms; to *Deal* in the way of traffic or merchandize, and, as I think, *Dale* and *Dell*, a valley. Before the enclosures in Lincolnshire the word *Dale* was frequently used to describe the shares of land which the freeholders and copyholders had in the open fields; this word was constantly employed when the portions of land were in such positions that they could not in any way be considered as valleys, *e.g.*, Dimmore dale, Bachester dale, Northorpe gate dale, Black moulde dale, Baytinge cross dale, Dale extra bori*alem* de slump cross, Beacon dale, Mount dale, and 2 dales iux*ta* molendin*um*, in the parish of Kirton in Lindsey.—Norden and Thorpe's Survey of Kirton Soke, *MS. Pub. Lib. Cantab.* Ff. 4, 30. fol. 7.

"So þat þe meste *del* of hey men þat in Englond beþ
Beþ ycome of þe Normans."

Rob. Glouc. 368.

"His mayster loved hym so welle,
He fette hym gold every *delle*."

Child of Bristow, Retrosp. Rev. Feb. 1854, p. 204.

"*Deal* on, *deal* on, my merry men, all
Deal on your cake and your wine,
For whatever is *dealt* at her funeral day,
Shall be dealt to-morrow at mine."

Marg. and Will., Percy Reliques.

"He turn'd his face unto the wa'
And death was with him *dealan*,
Adiew! adiew! my dear friends a'
Be kind to Barbara Allan."

Sir John Grehene and Barbara Allan, Percy's Reliques.

P. 18, l. 582. The holy oils used in the Catholic Church were of three kinds—*oleum sanctum, oleum chrismatis, et oleum infirmorum.* With the *oleum sanctum*, the creme of the text, the child was anointed on the breast and between the shoulders, during the introductory part of the baptismal service, ere it was plunged in the font or sprinkled with water. When the baptism proper was over it was anointed on the head in the form of a cross with *oleum chrismatis* or creme. The *oleum infirmorum*, or sick men's oil, was the oil used in the service of extreme unction. The oil used for this purpose was made from olives. With the chrism was mingled sweet smelling balsam. The consecration took place on Holy Thursday.—Maskell, *Mon. Rit.* i. 22. Rock, *Ch. of our Fathers*, iij. pt. ij. p. 79. The three little bottles in which these oils were preserved were kept in a box called a chrismatory. This little chest was usually oblong in form, with a crested lid, somewhat like the Noah's Arks children are wont to play with. It was often called an oynting-box, oil-box, or creme-box.

P. 19, l. 585. *Ore*, grace, mercy. Old Norse, *eira.*

> "Cryde hym mylce & *ore*."
> *Rob. Glouc.* 381.

P. 20, l. 651. *ȝerne*, earnestly. A.S. *Georne.*

> "He bed him *ȝerne* vor to a bide."
> *Rob. Glouc.* 487.

P. 21, l. 654. The sacrament of confirmation can, in ordinary cases, be administered by a bishop only. In some instances this power has been delegated to a priest. At these times the oil has been blessed by one of the episcopal order.

l. 660. *Stoke.* A.S. *Stoc*, a stake, from *stingan*, to thrust in, to prick, to sting. Dut. and Ger. *Stock.* Fr. *Estoc.* Ital. *Stocco.* Lat. *Truncus.* Hence, *Holy-Water-Stock*, the pillar or post on which the holy-water vessel was fixed. The *Stocks*, an instrument of correction. *Stocks*, the frame on which a ship is built. *Stocks*, public monies. *Stock*, a race or family. *Stock*, the store or fixed things on a farm. *Stock*, the stiff bandage round the neck. To *stock*, a North Country word for to bar or bolt a door. *Stock-Lock*, a lock fixed upon a door. *Stock*, the handle of any thing. *Stook*, twelve sheaves of corn *stuck* upright, their upper ends inclining towards each other like a high-pitched roof. *Stock-Dove*, the dove that lives in trees. *Stoothes*, thin spars of wood used in house building. *Stoccade*, a fence of stakes. *Stock*, a gilliflower, so called, says Skinner, "quia tum radix tum caulis instar ligni solida et dura sunt." *Stoker*, a man who sticks, *i.e.* pushes, pokes, or stirs the fire. *Stockfish*, so called "quia durus est instar *Stocci, i.e.* Trunci seu Caudicis," or because it is so hard that it requires beating with a stick to make it fit for eating. *Stocken*, a Lincolnshire word, signifying stopped in growth, choked with food or filled with water, as a sponge; and the family names of *Stock*, *Stocks*, and *Stookes*.

"A hallie water *stocke* of stone at the church dore with a sprinckle of a stick."—1566. *Ch. Goods Destroyed at Gretford.* Peacock's *Ch. Furniture*, 91.

[1579] "Payd to James battman xij*s*. ix*d*., by the collectors, for the poore, wich was layd owt of the common *stook* befor for Gouldes childe."—*Kirton in Lindsey Ch. Accts.* p. 71.

[1419] "In xxiiij. paribus ligaturarum ferri cum uncis et V *stokloks* ab eodem emptis, 10*s*. 4*d*."—*Fabric Rolls of York Minster*, 38.

[1519] "Oftyn tymes the dure is *stokked*, and we parsons & vicars cannot get brede, wyne, nor water."—*Ibid.* 268.

[1641] "Those that binde and *stooke* are likewise to have 8*d*. a day, for bindinge and *stookinge* of winter corne is a man's labour."—Best's *Farming Book*, 43.

[1552–3] "For settinge in ij. *stothes* and mendyng the wall of the receiver's chalmer over the stare."—Howden Roll, 5–6 Edward VI. Quoted in *Fabric Rolls of York Minster*, 355.

P. 21, l. 663. The person confirmed was anointed with chrism, in the form of a cross; afterwards, out of reverence for the chrism, the forehead was bandaged with a white linen band. The *Ordo Romanus* provides that this ligature should be worn for seven days. This was supposed to shadow forth the seven-fold gifts of the Holy Ghost, conferred by the rite; "Spiritus sapientiæ et intellectus, Spiritus consilii et fortitudinis, Spiritus scientiæ et pietatis et Spiritus timoris Domini." The length of time these fillets were retained varied in different places. The Council of Worcester, A.D. 1240, provided that they should be worn but three days. This is stated to have been in honour of the Trinity. They were to be removed in church by the priest, who was instructed to wash the foreheads of the confirmed, and to pour the water into the font. The bandages were usually ordered to be burnt. In some cases, however, it seems that they were reserved to be used as napkins for the priest to wipe his hands upon after using the holy oils. "Vero ad humanos usus nullatenus transferatur, sed comburatur, vel in usus muridos ecclesiæ deputetur." This passage is glossed, "Forte ad abstergendas manus post sacrorum oleorum contrectationem."—Martene, *De Antiq. Eccl. Rit.* i. 92; iv. 417.

P. 23, l. 733. *Flotterer*, a ship-man, a sailor. A.S. *Flota*, a ship; *Flot-here*, a body of seamen; *Flot-mann*, a sailor. Low. Ger. *Flote*, a raft. Fr. *Flotte*, a fleet. *Flotson* or *Flotsam* "is when a ship is drowned or othewise perished, & the goods float vpon the sea, & they are giuen to the Lord Admirall by his letters patents," *Les Termes de la Ley. cf.* Cowell's *Dict. sub voc.* *Flote*-grass or *Flotter*-grass, gramen fluviatile, so called because it floats upon the water.—Skinner, *Etymolog. sub voc.* *Prompt. Parv.* i. 168. Gerarde's *Herbal*, 1636, p. 14. In Lincolnshire we now call this weed Wreck.

P. 24, l. 766. Certain chapels and monasteries of royal foundation were exempt from ordinary jurisdiction. The authorities of these places were responsible for their acts to Rome only, and the priests therein were permitted, as an especial privilege, to celebrate marriages and hear the confessions of persons who were unconnected with the establishments. Battle Abbey, Waltham Abbey, the priory of St. Oswald of Nostell, co. York, and St. Martin's Church, London, were privileged places. See du Fresne, *Gloss. sub voc. Capella.*

P. 24, l. 782. *Wlatyng*, loathing, disgust. A.S. *Wlætung*, *wlatung*.

"Vorzoþe and zuo heþ god grat wlatiynge to ham þet ine þese þinges habbeþ blisse."—*Ayenbite of Inwyt*, 216.

P. 25, l. 795. *Fulhelt*, most probably. *Helt* in the dialects of Lancashire means likely, probable, perhaps. Halliw. *Dict.* O.N. *helzt.* Dan. *helst*, mostly in a high degree, most frequently, superlative of *heldr*, rather.

P. 26, l. 827. When our Lord was represented as Judge, the instincts of the mediæval artists told them that it was fitting that they should show the wounds in His sacred hands and feet. Most churches had in them, either frescoed on the walls, carved in stone, or stained in the windows, a picture of the doom. It was one of the commonest sights that met the eyes of the men and women of the Middle Ages, and thus

"hys woundys fresche and rede,"

the tokens of His boundless love, became also the symbols of His justice. Violence and neglect have deprived us of nearly all these outward manifestations of our fathers' piety and faith. Where it has been attempted to replace them, the old childlike and mystic spirit has been usually wanting.

Perhaps the grandest representation of the Lord Jesus as Judge which the world possesses, is the figure painted by Orcagna in the Campo Santo of Pisa. He is seated upon a rainbow within an ovoidal aureole, clad in sumptuous vestments with a tiara, as the sign of the highest spiritual sovereignty, upon his brows. The attitude of the figure is pacific and benevolent, but of terrible majesty. The right hand, the sign of power, is raised, not in menace, but in love, to show the print of the nail in its palm; with the left—the hand of mercy—He draws away His robe to show the cruel spear-stab in His side. The skirts of the garment are so arranged as to reveal a part—not the whole—of the wound in each foot.

P. 27, l. 862.

"She is abused, stolen from me and corrupted,
By spells and medicines bought of mountebanks."

Othello, i. 3.

Drinks to enforce lechery have been in use from the most remote recorded antiquity to the present time. See Burton's *Anat. Mel. Pt.* iii. *Sc.* 2, *Memb.* iii. *Subst.* 5, and the numberless books he quotes. See also Geo. K. Horst's *Zauberbibliothek*, and Colin de Plancy, *Dict. Infernale.* Newton, in his *Tryall of a man's owne selfe*, 12mo. Lond.

1602, p. 116, as quoted in Ellis's Brand's *Antiq.* ij. 603, asks, under the head of breaches of the seventh commandment, whether "By any secret sleight, or cunning, as Drinkes, Drugges, Medicines, charmed Potions, Amatorious, Philters, figures, characters, or any such like paltering Instruments, Devices, or Practises, thou hast gone about to procure others to doate for love of thee." This seems to be little more than a quotation from some Catholic book of examinations for confession.

These charms were not intended to procure sexual love alone. There is a shocking case on record of a Miss Mary Blandy, the daughter of a solicitor at Henley-on-Thames, who in the year 1751 was the cause of her father's death by giving to him a certain white powder—most probably arsenic—which her lover, a certain Captain William Henry Cranstoun, had sent her for that purpose, making her believe that it was a love-potion, and that its effect would be to make Mr. Blandy favourable to Cranstoun's addresses to his daughter. The poor woman was tried for murder in the Divinity School at Oxford, on the 9th of March, 1752, and hanged on the Castle-green on the 6th of April following.—*Gent. Mag.* xxi. 376, 486; xxij. 108, 116, 152, 188. There is a list of the pamphlets relating to this horrible case in Bohn's Loundes' *Bibl. Manual.*

P. 29, l. 934. *Kynde*, semen.—Chaucer, *Parson's Tale*, ed. Morris, iij. 355.

l. 942. *Hele*, hide, cover, conceal. A.S. *Hélan.*

"And *helud* shal ben wiþ a cloþ."

Signs of Death in Polit. Relig. and Love Poems, p. 224, l. 2.

"Be it made to him a cloþe þat he is *helid* wiþ, and as belt þat is he ai gird wiþ."—Wicliffe's [?] *Lollard Doctrines*, Camd. Soc. p. 24.

[1473] "ij. kerchyvys for to *hele* the sacrament."—Boy's *Sandwich*, 374.

P. 32, l. 1033. Our ancestors, like children, delighted in bright and strongly contrasted colours. Party-coloured garments were very common. They frequently, though not always, had an heraldic signification. In some highly interesting illuminations representing the Courts of Law of the time of Henry VI., published by the late Mr. Corner, in the *Archæologia*, v. 39, p. 357, the serjeants and most of the officials are represented in party-coloured robes. When Charles first Duke of Manchester went as ambassador to Venice [1696 or 1707], his servants wore liveries of this kind. What was once an honourable costume became in time, by a process of degradation well known to antiquaries, the badge of a degrading office. In quite modern days the executioner at Palermo was clad, when on duty, in a party-coloured dress of red and yellow.—*Ibid.* 372.

P. 33, l. 1062. *Drawe on tret*, drawn out, drawn at length, come to a point. I have not met with the phrase elsewhere.

P. 36, l. 1175. *Wedde*, a pledge. A.S. *Wed* (from Goth. *With-an*, to join, to bind). Dut. *Wedde.* Belg. *Wedden.* Hence *Wed*, to marry. *Wedding*, *Wedlock*. *Wedbedrip*, the customary service under-tenants paid to their lords in cutting corn and other harvest works.

"1325. Robertus Filius Nicholai Germayn tenet unum messuagium & dimidiam virgatam in bondagio ad voluntatem Domini & debet unam aruram in Yeme & unam sarculaturam & debet *Wedbedrip* pro voluntate Domini."—*Paroch. Antiquit.* 401 in Cowel, *sub voc.*

Wadset, a mortgage. A Scottish law term. Sandford's *Treatise on Entails in Scotl.* 262.

P. 38, l. 1216. All men were not bound to fast to the same degree, or in the same manner. The fasts of the monastic orders were harder to bear than those of lay people, and the monks differed much among themselves in the severity, order, and frequency of their fasts. Each diocese had its own rules, so that it sometimes happened that the dwellers on one side of a street were merrily feasting, while those on the other were mortifying themselves on fish. This was the case in Cheapside, in the sixteenth century, where one row of the houses happened to be in the diocese of Canterbury and the opposite one in that of London (Pilkington's *Works*, *Parker Soc.*, 557). Bishops had authority in their respective dioceses to grant dispensations from all fasts. The Crown seems to have exercised a co-ordinate jurisdiction. Several licences not to fast may be found on the Patent Rolls, and memoranda relating to the same order of things may be found in many other places among our public records, *e.g.*, in 1222 or 1223, John the son of Henry was indebted to the king in four marks "pro licentia comedendi," half of which sum he had paid into the treasury, and the rest was still owing (*Mag. Rot.* 7, *H.* 3, *Rot.* 11, *a. Everw.*, as quoted in Madox, *Hist. Exchequer*, 1711, p. 353). Licences of this sort continued to be in use long after the Reformation; one dated 9th February, 1580–1, is preserved, by which the Archbishop of Canterbury, Edmund Grindal, permits Sir Edward Verney, of Penley, Knight, to eat flesh on days forbidden, for the term of his life, on the ground that a diet of fish disagreed with him; he received also the additional favour of being permitted to share these pleasures of the table with his wife and any three other persons whom he might select (*Verney Papers*, 85). A similar licence, by Thomas Westfield, S.T.D., rector of the church of St. Bartholomew the Great, London, granted in the year 1639 to Mrs. Mary Anthony, wife of John Anthony, of the same parish, Doctor of "Phisick," was printed at length in the *Gentleman's Magazine* for April, 1812, p. 314. The churchwardens of this parish received on behalf of the poor for licences such as these i*l.* vj*s.* viij*d.* from noblemen, and vj*s.* viij*d.* from those of lower degree. In Scotland it would seem that after the Reformation these licences were granted by the civil power, without even a pretence of ecclesiastical authority.—*Ibid.* p. 24.

l. 1240. *Sybbe*, akin. A.S. *Sib*, *Gesibb*.

"A woman may in no lesse sinne assemble with her *Godsib*, than with her own fleshly father."—Chaucer, *Parson's Tale: De luxuria*.

"A Stuarts are na' *sib* to the king."—Scottish Proverb, Ramsay's *Scottish Life and Charac.* p. 145.

"By the religion of our holy church they are ower *sibb* thegither."—*Antiquary*, ch. xxxiii.

The word is still used in Lincolnshire, *e.g.*, "our Marmaduke is *sib* to all the gentles in the country, though he has come down to lead coals."—*Circa* 1856.

l. 1243. *Ankeras*, a female ankret. The ankrets were persons bound by vows to lead a solitary life. They usually dwelt in the church, sometimes in a little lodge adjoining. Their duty when in holy orders was to say mass, evensong, etc., and to assist the parochial clergy; probably also to clean the sacred vessels, and take care of the church furniture. The duties of the ankress were much the same as those of the ankret who was not in holy orders. She sometimes, though it would seem more rarely, lived within the church. In 1383 William de Belay, of Lincoln, left to an ankress named Isabella, who dwelt in the church of the Holy Trinity, in Wigford, within the city of Lincoln, 13*s*. 4*d*. In 1391 John de Sutton left her 20*s*.; in 1394 John de Ramsay left her 12*d*. Besides these she had numerous other legacies from dying citizens, who at that awful crisis were reminded (most touchingly, perhaps, by the severe mortification of one whom they had almost daily before their eyes) of the higher life and narrower way which they in health and prosperity had shrunk from or forgotten. In 1453 an ankress named Matilda supplied the place of Isabella, who, we may suppose, had long since gone to her reward. In that year John Tilney, one of the Tilneys of Boston (see ped. in Thompson's *Hist.* 373), left "Domine Matilde incluse infra ecclesiam Sancte Trinitatis ad gressus in civitate Lincoln, vj*s*. viij*d*." In 1502 Master John Watson, a chaplain [capellanus] in Master Robert Flemyng's Chantry, left xij*d*. to the ankers [ankress?] at the Greese Foot. This church of the Holy Trinity, "ad gressus," seems to have been for a long period the abode of a female recluse. It was called "ad gressus" on account of standing at the bottom of the steep flight of stairs by which men ascended from the lower to the higher city. A street or highway, called the New-road, now passes over the once hallowed spot. The remains of those who slept within its inclosure have, I believe, been dispersed. The steps from which the church took its name are now named the Greecen or Greetstone Stairs. In Norfolk stairs are called *grissens*. I am informed they are still spoken of as *grices* in Lincolnshire, but have myself never heard the word. It was not obsolete here in 1566.

"The steers or *gryses* coming vpp to the altare."
Mon. Sup. Folkingham, in Peacock's *Ch. Fur.* 81.

John Haster, a goldsmith, kept a shop at "the mynster gresses," at York, in 1510. He was presented at the visitation for having suspicious persons in his house at "unconvenient tymes."—*Detecta Quædam in Visitat. Ebor.*, Surtees Soc., 35, p. 262.

Thomas Hearne has printed an episcopal commission, dated 1402, for shutting up John Cherde, a monk of Ford Abbey.—Trokelowe's *Annals*, 263. It would seem that an episcopal licence was necessary ere a man or woman could assume this manner of life. Richard Francis, an ankret, is spoken of as "inter quatuor parietes pro Christo inclusus."—Langt. *Chron.* ij. 625.

P. 39, l. 1253. *Clyppynge*, embracing, hugging. A.S. *Clyppan*, to embrace.

> "Quaþ blauncheflur ich com anon,
> Ac floriz *cleppen* here bigon."
>
> *Floris and Blanchf.* 67, 594.

> "To *clippen* & kissen they counten in tounes,
> The damoseles that to the daunce sewe."
>
> *Plowman's Tale*, edit. 1687, p. 165.

A Lincolnshire peasant said to the editor, concerning one of her neighbours, that "She *clipped* and cuddled the bairn as thof she'd never seen it sin Candlemas." (We still talk here of 'sheep-clipping' for sheep-shearing.) *Clip*, to cut, shear, is O.N. *Klippa.*

P. 42, l. 1346. The holy-bread, the holy-loaf, or eulogia, was ordinary leavened bread cut into small pieces, blessed, and given to the people after mass was over. The idea entertained by some persons at the period of the Reformation, and in subsequent times, that this rite was instituted as a substitute for the Holy Communion is erroneous. Modern writers have sometimes even confounded the two. Holy bread had nothing sacramental in its nature: it was used in the manner of the ancient love-feasts as a type of the Christian fellowship that should exist among those who were of the household of faith. This practice was once almost universal in Western Christendom, and prevailed to some extent among the Greeks, where it was called Αντίδωρα. It has now gone entirely out of use in this country. I believe, however, it is still distributed in some of the dioceses of France. Thomas Becon, Archbishop Cranmer's chaplain, speaks of it in his catechism. He says that "because the people should not be altogether without some outward thing to put them in remembrance of the body-breaking and blood-shedding of Christ, the Papists have brought into the Church two ceremonies, that is to say, *holy-bread* and holy-water; and they every Sunday minister them to the common people instead of the honourable sacrament of the body and blood of Christ, by giving them the bread to eat, and by casting the water on their faces." It was customary in early times for the receivers to carry home this "panis benedictus." It was said that in the fifteenth century some people used to employ it as a charm, and on that account carry it about their persons. One of Cranmer's articles of enquiry, published in the second year of Edward VI., is, "whether any person hath abused the ceremonies, as in casting holy water upon his bed, or bearing about him *holy bread*, St. John's Gospel, ringing of holy bells, or keeping of private holy days, as tailors, bakers, brewers, smiths, shoemakers, and such other."

One of the demands of the Devonshire men, who, in 1549, rose in arms to fight for the restoration of the old religion, was that they might "have *holy-bread* and holy-water every Sunday." The martyrologist Foxe gives us the words which Hugh Latimer was wont to use when he distributed the holy loaf to his flock:—

"Of Christ's body this is the token,
Which on the cross for your sins was broken;
Wherefore of your sins you must be forsakers,
If of Christ's death ye will be partakers."

It was decreed by the Constitutions of Giles de Bridport, Bishop of Salisbury, A.D. 1254, that the parishioners should provide the holy loaf every Sunday. The order in which it was provided in the parish of Stanford-in-the-Vale, co. Berks., may be seen from an extract from the church account book of that parish, published by Dr. Rock.

There were "ij. *hally-brede* basckatts" among the goods belonging to St. Olave's, Southwark, in 1558. In 1566, at Gonwarby, in Lincolnshire, "one *hally brede* skeppe [was] sold to Mr. Allen, and he maketh a baskett to carrie ffishe in."

In the Sacristy of St. Andrew, at Vercelli, is still preserved a curious knife with a box-wood handle, carved with the occupations of each month of the year. This instrument is thought to have been intended for cutting the blessed bread. It has an additional interest to Englishmen from the fact that it is believed to have once belonged to St. Thomas of Canterbury.—Bingham's *Antiq.* ed. 1834, v. 300, 322. Rock's *Ch. of our Fathers*, i. 135–140. Becon's *Catech.* ed. 1844, 260. Cranmer's *Works*, ed. Fox, ii. 158, 503. Wilkins' *Conc.* i. 714. Peacock's *Ch. Fur.* 86, 96. *Gent. Mag.* 1837, i. 492. Hart's *Eccl. Records*, 205, 294.

l. 1353. *Lychwake.* A.S. *lic*, a body; *wæccan*, to watch. The Lake-wake or Lyke-wake was the watching of the corpse, common among all simple-minded people. It arose out of some of the holiest instincts of our nature, but has at all times been liable to foul corruption. We have ample evidence that these death watchings often degenerated in the Middle Ages into riotous festivals. The custom is not extinct in Ireland, Scotland, or Sweden. I believe it still lingers in the Northern Shires of England. John Aubrey has preserved in his *Remains of Gentilisme & Judaisme*, Lansd. MS. 231, fol. 114, an account of these festivous funeral rites taken from the lips of "Mr. Mawtese, in whose fathers youth s*cilicet* about 60 yeares since [1686 now] at country vulgar Funeralls was sung this song."

"At the Funeralls in Yorkshire to this day they continue the custome of watching & sitting vp all night till the Body is interred. In the interim some kneel downe and pray (by the corps), some play at cards, some drink & take Tobacco: they have also Mimicall playes & sports, *e.g.* they choose a simple young fellow to be a Judge, then the Suppliants (having first blacked their hands by rubbing it under the bottome of the Pott) beseech his Lo*rdshi*p and smutt all his face.

they play likewise at Hott-cockles.

. . . . . .

The beleefe in Yorkshire was amongst the vulgar•(& p*er*haps is in part still) that after the parsons death, the Soule went over Whinnimore, and till about $\frac{1624}{1616}$ at thė Funerall a woman came [like a Præfica], and sung the following Song:—

This ean night, this ean night,
  eve[r]y night and awle:
Fire and Fleet[1] and Candle-light,
  and Christe recieve thy Sawle.
When thou from hence doest pass away,
  every night and awle,
To Whinny-moore thou comest at last,
  and Christ recieve thy[2] Sawle.
If ever thou gave either hosen or shun,
  every night and awle,
Sitt thee downe and putt them on,
  and Christ recieve thy Sawle.
But if hosen nor shoon thou never gave nean,
  every night, etc.
The Whinnes[3] shall prick thee to the bare beane,
  and Christ recieve thy Sawle.
From Whinny-moor that thou mayst pass,
  every night, etc.
To Brig o' Dread, thou comest at last,
  and Christ, etc.,
      no brader than a thread. [fol. 114 *b*.]
From Brig of Dread that thou mayst pass,
  every night, etc.
To Purgatory fire thou com'st at last,
  and Christ, etc.
If ever thou gave either Milke or drinke,
  every night, etc.
The fire shall never make thee shrink,
  and Christ, etc.

[1] water.

[2] 'silly, poor,' *interlined.*

[3] Furze.

But if milk nor drink thou never gave nean,
every night, etc.
The Fire shall burn thee to the bare bene,
and Christ recieve thy Sawle."

A version of this strange dirge, varying in a few minute particulars, was printed by Sir Walter Scott in his *Minstrelsy of the Scottish Border* (edit. 1861, ii. 135–142). I should have imagined that it had been derived from the same MS. as the above, had not Sir Walter spoken of it in such a manner as to induce us to believe that it was still the custom to sing it at funerals when he made his great collection of oral poetry. His words are—"This is a sort of charm sung by the lower rank of Roman Catholics in some parts of the north of England, while watching a dead body previous to interment. The tune is doleful and monotonous, and joined to the mysterious import of the words has a solemn effect."

It is possible that these verses may yet linger as a tradition among the peasantry of the North of England. If so, it is much to be desired another copy should be procured. The above is evidently corrupted in several places.

In an account of some matters relating to the neighbourhood of Gisborough, written about the end of the sixteenth century by a correspondent of Sir Thomas Challoner, who signed himself H. Tr . . . . , we have the following curious picture. There cannot be much doubt that the "songe" which "certaine women singe" was of the same nature as, if not identical with, the verses preserved by John Aubrey.

"When any dieth certaine women singe a songe to the dead body, recytinge the iorney that the p*ar*tie deceased must goe, and they are of beleife (such is their fondnesse) that once in their liues yt is good to giue a payre of newe shoes to a poore man, forasmuch as after this life they are to passe barefoote through a greate launde full of thornes & furzen, excepte by the meryte of the Almes aforesaide, they have redemed their forfeyte: for at the edge of the launde an aulde man shall meete them w*i*th the same shoes that were giuen by the p*ar*tie when he was liuinge, and after he hath shodde them he dismisseth them to goe through thicke and thin w*i*thout scratch or scalle."—Cotton MS. *Julius*, F. vi. fol. 438*b*.

P. 43, l. 1385. The ecclesiastical councils of Christendom have frequently prohibited unclean beasts being allowed to feed in churchyards. In some parts of Denmark the intrusion of cattle in graveyards is prevented by an iron grating being fixed in the gateway, under which a deep hole has been excavated. Over this men and women can walk with ease, but sheep and pigs are unable to do so as their feet slip between the bars.—Hamilton's *Sixteen Months in the Danish Isles*, i. 135.

P. 43, l. 1391.

> "Now turn again, turn again, said the Pinder,
> For a wrong way you have gone, &c.,
> For you have forsaken the kings highway,
> And made a path over the corn," &c.
>
> *The Pinder of Wakefield & Robin Hood.*

There was in former days a very strong feeling of dislike against those persons who trod down growing corn. The sentiment was more intense than the mere money loss warranted. In times when famines were probable contingencies, people realized more fully than they do now the wickedness of destroying human food. The feeling has happily not as yet died out among our rural poor.

P. 48, l. 1546. *Quede*, wicked = the devil. Dutch, *Quade*, evil.

> "He so haveth of fur mest, he schal beo smal and red,
> other blak with crips her, lene, and somdel *qued*."
>
> *Pop. Treatises on Science*, 138.

> "And lete me neuere falle
> In boondis to the *queed*."
>
> *Hymns to Virg. and Christ*, p. 6, l. 18.

l. 1559. Dead men's bones, corpses in process of decay, worms devouring putrid bodies, and similar subjects, were objects of frequent contemplation to our forefathers. The abbots of the Carthusian order, when in chapter, had a human skull laid before them. Many mediæval monuments survive where the deceased is represented as an emaciated corpse or a fleshless skeleton.—See *Notes and Queries*, 1st series, v. 247, 301, 353, 427, 497; vi. 85, 252, 321, 345, 393, 445, 520; vii. 429. Douce's Holbein's *Dance of Death*, *passim*. Shakespere had evidently been deeply affected by such like objects of contemplation.

P. 50, l. 1607. This shows that the author took it for granted that there would be in every church a sanctus bell, which would be rung to turn men's thoughts to God at the moment of consecration.

P. 51, l. 1651. *Ȝop*, wary. A.S. *Geap*, crooked, deceitful, cunning.

> "He stiȝtleȝ stif in stalle
> Ful ȝep in þat nw zere."
>
> *Sir Gawayne and the Green Knight*, p. 4, l. 104.

P. 55, l. 1760. *Hull*, cover. A.S. *Hélan*. The act of shelling beans or peas, or removing the outer husk of walnuts, is called *hulling* in Lincolnshire. Pods or husks are *hulls*.

P. 56, l. 1825. *Coppe*, a spider. A.S. *Attercoppa*, literally a poison head, cup, or bag. Cobweb is a corruption of coppe-web. There is a wonderful tale in the preface to Hearne's Langtoft's *Chron*. p. cc., of three persons being poisoned by the venom of an *atturcoppe*, of whom two died, and the third was so near death that he made his will, and in all other ways got ready for his departure, when, happening to think of Saint Winefrede and of the miracles wrought by her, he induced his mother to go to her shrine and offer a candle there, and "brynge hym of þe water þat her bones were wasschon yn." With the use of this water he soon recovered, and as a thank-offering he presented at her shrine an image of silver. The account does not say what the image represented. I presume it was a figure either of himself or of the saint who had helped him; perhaps the spider also was shewn.—See *Prompt. Parv. sub voc.* Richardson's *Dict. sub Cobweb.*

GLOSSARIAL INDEX.

	PAGE.	LINE.
A-bregge, abridge,	47	1517
A-bygge, abide,	59	1898
A-corset, accursed,	23	736
A-ferd, frightened. Still used in North Lincolnshire,	41	1335
A-go, gone,	35	1140
Al-gate, anyhow, always,	44	1414
	45	1448
	55	1766
Als, as	13	394
	29	944
An-elet, anointed	53	1700
Ankeras, Ankress, Anchoress, a female hermit,	38	1243
	45	1447
Annoynted,	21	670
A-nont, upon	57	1849
A-pert, openly,	41	1336
Artykele, article,	15	458
Aster, Easter,	5	143
	8	241
At ene, at once,	3	82
A-tent, intent,	26	841
Auter, altar,	54	1755
A-vow, A-voue, vow,	13	396
A-vys, advice,	8	226
Axtree, axletree,	11	334
Ay, ever,	14	452
Aȝte, ought,	45	1444
Backbyte, backbiting,	36	1155
Baldely, plainly,	32	1020
Baselard, a dagger,	2	48
Bawdryke, a belt,	2	48
Be-bled, blodied,	56	1822
Beleue, belief,	12	366
Ben, be,	17	524
Benefyces, benefits,	10	317
Bere, noise, uproar,	8	240
	9	276, 289
Be-stad, bestood, circumstanced,	42,	1362
Bete, make better = heal, save, cure,	16	515
Beth, be,	1	6
Bifor, before,	16	n.
Blyue, quickly,	13	394
	40	1306
Bollyng, bull-baiting,	11	n.
Bondes,	21	663
Boo, both,	1	3
Bordes, jests, games,	9	267
	19	588
	37	1213

	PAGE.	LINE.
Brenne, burn,	4	116
Brenner, burner,	51	1655
By-dene, presently, at once,	55	1758
By-forn, before,	16	519
By-gylet, beguiled,	37	1187
Byspyng, bishoping = confirmation,	20	646
By-taghte, taught,	45	1468
By-twynne, between,	7	220
Candell,	55	1763
Caste,	33	1070
Casteth, plots, contrives,	46	1483
Castynge, vomiting,	58	1888
Chafare, merchandize, exchange, barter. A.S. *ceáp*, a bargain. Hence the family name *Chaffers*,	37	1187
Chames, charms, spells,	12	368
Chast, chaste	2	23
Chaunge, change,	20	638
Chost, strife,	11	338
	42	1365
Churchay, churchyard. A.S. *cyrice*, church. *Heg*, hay, grass, or *hege*, a hedge or fence,	11	n.
Chyrche, church,	17	527
Clanseþ, cleanseth,	17	528
Cloyserere, cloisterer = monk, canon,	44	1411
Clypping, embracing = cutting, clipping,	39	1253
Comyn wommon, harlot,	38	1246
Confermynge,	17	529
Conne, know,	1	16
Connynge, knowing,	43	1400
Contrycyone,	47	1512
Coppe, spider. A.S. *attercoppa*, a spider, *lit.* a poison head, poison bag, or poison cup,	56	1825
Corporas, a linen cloth used in the service of the mass,	56	1810
Cosynage, cousinhood, relationship	6	168
Cotteyng, quoiting, playing at quoits,	11	n.
Couetyse, covetousness	36	1169
Counter, contrary,	48	1553
Court,	24	766
Couth, known,	24	n.
Cowpulle, copulation,	7	194
Cowþe, could,	20	619
Creawance, credence,	52	1676
Creme, holy oil,	18	582
	20	634
Crome, crumb,	59	1901
Croys, cross,	14	437
Crysme, holy oil,	18	582
Cunnen, can,	8	237
Curatowre, curate,	28	912
Dawe, days,	1	5
Ded, death,	8	247
Deden, did,	18	556
Dedeyn, disdain,	32	1047
Dedlyche, deadly,	30	969
Dele, part,	16	499
Deme, sentence,	17	523
Derrur, dearer,	12	383
Despuyte, dispute,	21	673
Destruye, destroy,	35	1128
Deuors, divorce,	7	197
Disturbul, disturb,	62	4
Domes-day,	16	521
Drawe on tret,	33	1062
Droken, drunken,	20	631
Dronkelec, Dronkelewe, drunkenness,	2	31
Dronken,	20	623
Dryȝt, the Lord Jesus Christ. A.S. *drihten*,	14	426
Dyuynyte,	15	456
Dyȝte, dispose = deck adorn. A.S. *dihtan*,	54	1755

	PAGE.	LINE.
Laten, Latin,	18	570
Layne, reward,	22	698
	43	1398
Lechery,	44	1436
Lechowre,	40	1282
Ledeth hys lyf, gains his living,	24	760
Lemmon, concubine,	23	719
Lene, lend,	43	1373
Lentenes-day, Easter	3	75
Lere, teach. A.S. *lǽran*,	17	546
Lered, learned = clergy,	35	1146
Lese, lose,	10	325
Lesyng, falsehood,	30	953
Leue, believe,	9	260
	15	459
Leue, leave	8	259
Lewd, lay,	20	645
Lewte, loyalty,	28	913
Loke, locked,	21	660
Londes, land,	32	1035
Lone, loan,	12	383
Lust, list,	22	708
Lutte, light,	48	1547
Luyte, light, little, 40 1304;	51	1635
	36	1156
Luytel, littel,	20	627
Lychwake, the watching of the corpse before burial,	42	1353
Lyde ȝate, lych gate,	43	1385
Lyet, lied,	30	953
Lyth, the body,	39	1253
Madhede, madness,	48	1545
Male, a budget, a satchel = the belly,	38	1230
Malencholy,	36	1157
May, maid,	38	1239
Mayde,	24	783
Mayn, haste, force,	37	1203
Mede, meed, reward,	46	1476
Meyne, company = servant,	34	1084
Mischawnce, mischance,	59	1899
Mo, more,	17	534
Mod, mood,	24	772
Mon, man,	4	105
Monslaȝt, manslaughter,	44	1423
Mot, much,	45	1466
Mowe, may,	4	95
Myche, much,	21	679
Mynge, mingle = mind, remember, observe. A.S. *mengian*,	45	1443
	59	1915
Mynne, remember,	8	233
	17	529
Myscheueth, unfortunate, ill, happen, an accident,	17	550
Myȝt, mighty,	15	461
Nedely, necessarily. *Needlings* is still a Lincolnshire word,	13	401
Negh, nigh,	23	743
Nere, ne were = were not,	20	620
	21	671
Nete, neat = horned cattle,	11	353
Neur the latter, never the less,	3	87
	8	250
Newe, accrue, come by growth,	11	348
Newed, renewed,	20	642
	45	1463
Neȝ, near,	47	1520
Nome, name,	17	551
	45	1439
Nonne, nun,	38	1243
Nother, } neither,	36	1171
Nowþer, }	12	386
Nuye, annoy. O.F. *anoi*, from Lat. *odium*,	4	120
Ny, nor,	18	565
Nym, take = comprehend,	17 n.	
Nyste, ignorance. A.S. *nyste*, do not know, from *nitan* (*ne-witan*), not to know,	37	1209

	PAGE.	LINE.
Wry, turn away,	24	776
Wrynge, wring,	24	780
Wyntynge, witting=knowledge,	13	397
Wys, wise,	20	628
Wyte, wit=know,	43	1403
Wyþ-say, deny, withhold,	36	1180
Wyth-tan, withdrawn, withheld,	37	1185
Wytte, knowledge,	8 n.	
Ydul, idle,	12	356
Yeke, the same. Sc. *ilk*,	10	322
	30	968
Yen, eyes,	24	771
Ypocryse, hypocrisy,	31	990
Yrke, irk,	19	526
Ys, is,	16	520
Ys, ice,	15	473

	PAGE.	LINE.
ȝaf, gave,	31	986
ȝates, gates. *Yate* is the Lincolnshire pronunciation,	16	489
ȝef, if,	3	86
ȝen, give,	21	683
ȝerne, earnestly. A.S. *georne*,	2	53
	3	70
ȝerus, years,	50	1626
ȝeue, give,	5	138
ȝeyn-stondynge, against standing=withstanding,	16	491
ȝonge, young,	9	286
ȝop, active,	51	1651
ȝore, sorely,	1	9
	37	1192
ȝow, you,	5	124
	15	470

PRINTED BY STEPHEN AUSTIN AND SONS, PRINTERS, HERTFORD.